General Systems Theory
Beginning with Wholes

D1248506

General Systems Theory
Beginning with Wholes

Barbara Gail Hanson
York University
Toronto, Ontario, Canada

Taylor & Francis
Publishers since 1798

USA	Publishing Office:	Taylor & Francis
		1101 Vermont Avenue, N.W., Suite 200
		Washington, D.C. 20005-3521
		Tel: (202) 289-2174
		Fax: (202) 289-3665
	Distribution Center:	Taylor & Francis
		1900 Frost Road, Suite 101
		Bristol, PA 19007-1598
		Tel: (215) 785-5800
		Fax: (215) 785-5515
UK		Taylor & Francis, Ltd.
		4 John St.
		London WC1N 2ET
		Tel: 071 405 2237
		Fax: 071 831 2035

GENERAL SYSTEMS THEORY BEGINNING WITH WHOLES

1 2 3 4 5 6 7 8 9 0   B R B R   9 8 7 6 5

This book was set in Times Roman by Sandra F. Watts. The editors were Lisa Speckhardt and Christine Williams. The pre-press supervisor was Bonny Gaston. Cover design by Michelle Fleitz. Printing and binding by Braun-Brumfield, Inc.

A CIP catalog record for this book is available from the British Library.
∞ The paper in this publication meets the requirements of the ANSI Standard Z39.48-1984 (Permanence of Paper).

Library of Congress Cataloging-in-Publication Data

Hanson, Barbara Gail.
   General systems theory beginning with wholes / Barbara Gail
Hanson.
     p. cm.
   Includes bibliographical references and index.

   1. System theory. I. Title.
Q295.H365 1995
003—dc20
                                      95-10543
                                          CIP
ISBN 1-56032-345-0 (cloth)
ISBN 1-56032-346-9 (paper)

Contents

Contents

Preface

I became enthralled by general systems theory early in my graduate career. It has grounded all my subsequent work and teaching. I wrote *General Systems Theory Beginning with Wholes* because I wanted to share the excitement and potential of systems ideas with a large audience. So much of what has been written about it before has been in the physical sciences or inaccessible prose in the behavioral sciences.

The importance of a general systems theory approach is not so much in its formal ideas as in the shift to a new way of seeing things. When I teach about systems theory I concentrate on encouraging students to make that shift by giving them multiple examples that tie into their own personal experiences or current events. Typically students make a leap into a systems mode of seeing and thinking when they realize that what seems complex and foreign at first is in fact intuitive to their lives. My favorite compliment as a teacher came one day when I overheard a student talking about my course. He said, "I'm not going to be able to live a normal life after taking this course." I like that.

Writing this book proved to be a difficult task. With other writing I have been describing something concrete and outside myself, but the uniqueness of a systems approach as a way of seeing meant the process was more like describing how to walk or breathe. I persevered, driven by the desire to make systems theory knowable, or perhaps more importantly "feel-able," to a wide audience in the hope that more people will use it.

This book is important to anyone working in the helping professions—counseling, nursing, therapy, social work—who has greeted systems theory at some point but may not have grasped it fully owing to the abstract nature of conventional systems writing. Academics who want to know about general systems theory in environmental studies, psychology, sociology, family therapy, social work, economics, history, nursing, social policy, marketing, or women's studies will find this book both comprehensive for their own libraries and useful in teaching. Students will find that this book reads like a good lecture, one which imparts ideas thoroughly and easily.

This book covers 31 general systems theory concepts that are directly relevant to the behavioral sciences: context, nonsummativity, system, unit, causality, cybernetics, action and inaction, co-emergence, agency, change, feedback, equifinality and multifinality, content, content and context, meaning, parallogic, realities, communication, report and command, you cannot not communicate, double bind, emotion, suprarationality, definitional deficit and definitional equality, science, multiverse, subjectivity, tools, data, decoding, and general constructs. Each concept is defined, explained, and illustrated on the personal, organizational, and social policy level. The derivations and significance are given to link each concept to its theoretical place and practical usage.

Long-time systems devotees will find themselves being updated by learning new "state of the art" systems concepts like action and inaction are equally causal, the impossibility of blame, multifinality, parallogic, realities, definitional deficit and definitional equality, content and context—light through a prism, multiverse, suprarationality, emotion, decoding and general constructs. They will also greet old favorites like system, nonsummativity, double bind, and feedback and cybernetics, explained in accessible language with extensions into organizations and social policy. The annotated bibliography provides a comprehensive list of significant systems ideas from Aristotle to sources in 1994.

The uninitiated will find a comfortable and informative path on which to begin to see and feel as a systems theorist and realize its particular relevance to issues like nuclear disarmament, AIDS, environmental degradation, anorexia, spouse abuse, senile dementia, and military action. Anyone who wants to appreciate seeing wholes as a means of innovating in their work will get not just the expanded view but all the references and examples they need to justify their new ideas.

ACKNOWLEDGMENTS

I owe my intellectual heritage to Norman W. Bell who taught me how to think without ever telling me what to think. That process is woven throughout this book.

Completion of this project was aided by support through my appointments as Visiting Scholar, Institute for Research on Women, Rutgers University, and Visiting Fellow, Department of Sociology, Princeton University.

Chapter 1

Introduction

Aristotle came up with the idea that the whole is greater than the sum of its parts. Alice discovered in Wonderland that meaning is relative to context. Anne of Green Gables shows us how emotion is the center of human experience. These three imaginings ground a "wholes" approach.

My purpose in writing this book is to give readers a feeling for the possibilities found in seeing the world in terms of wholes, or relational patterns. This means setting aside preconceived notions about how to begin inquiry that may restrict the range of phenomena brought into our scholarly viewing lenses. Though I will elaborate and give greater detail to this stance, its essence is as simple as allowing for the idea that there are things that emerge in groups of two or more parts that are not witnessed in those parts alone.

See that there is more to a child and parent together than when they are alone in separate rooms. Witness the process when a child falls and scrapes a knee, goes right on playing until the parent appears, and then begins crying. When a committee meets to decide on a course of action, such as which play to present for the summer festival, why is it that while all the individuals have excellent suggestions, the ultimate decision is in favor of something that no one likes? Has rent control, which was intended to increase the quality and availability of rental housing in Toronto, led to the reverse? Over time, a black market for securing housing in the form of "key money" co-emerged, along with grossly fluctuating markets for condominiums and escalating use of food banks. As capital shifted to expensive rental accommodation, people had to pay more for housing, and therefore had less to spend on food.

All of these examples point out that when we begin to see in terms of wholes rather than parts, patterns appear that a classic model of simple linear cause and effect cannot capture. They point out that such patterns, which we will learn later in this text can be described as "multifinal," can be found on any of the so-called levels that more conventional approaches cling to for analysis. There are patterned similarities between an intimate relationship that escalates into violence, a committee that decides to deny parole, and the escalation of the arms race leading ultimately to the Gulf War.

The idea of nonsummativity is not new. It can be traced back to Aristotle and the ancient Greek saying, "Never step in the same river twice for as it stays the same it is constantly changing." What is new is the potential of a wholes approach for transforming debate on current global problems through rethinking the epistemologies that ground conventional analysis. In this shift new visions appear for intervention. This arises by adding recent advances in wholes thinking about human groups to the basic tenets of a general systems theory approach developed largely in the physical sciences.

In addition to levels or sizes of groups of two or more parts, the content of the patterns analyzed is not restricted by a wholes approach. The Malpeque oysters of Prince Edward Island were once threatened by extinction due to widespread cancer but somehow overcame it. Computer viruses have been found and have become a common part of language in recent years. Gang swarming of shopping malls is getting increased attention. All of these events can be analyzed via the concept of "feedback." The ideas generated through a wholes or general systems theory approach can be used to consider any form of substantive issue where there are two or more interrelated parts. Because of this it is possible to think of the approach as "pan-disciplinary" in that it can be used across conventionally defined disciplines such as biology, computer science, engineering, sociology, economics, family therapy, medicine, or psychology.

In addition to transcending disciplinary boundaries, a wholes or systems approach cuts across conventionally defined theories. This is possible because a wholes approach is not set up like theories which begin with assumptions and derive their stances from these assumptions. In the conventional mode of making theories, because the applications and derivations hang directly from their assumptions, theories could not be compared or challenged across these assumptions. For example, the assumptions of human benevolence in Marx's writings, versus human greed and insatiability in Emile Durkheim's writings, make legitimate challenge of one by the other impossible in that one could not go beyond questioning the basic assumption about human nature each presents.

A wholes approach proposes to transcend this type of conventional debate by offering a way of seeing without the prescription of assumptions. Instead the point of departure that the whole is greater than the sum of its parts is offered. Wholes of whatever content or membership become the focus of analysis, leaving the individual to read on assumptions of choice while still using the language provided by a systems approach. As such it presents a new means of talking about a host of events and issues that moves beyond the discrete and linear and toward the whole and emergent.

This sets the stage for new modes of research, intervention, and policy that are informed by consideration of the long-term effects of actions that have traditionally been seen only as linear cause and effect sequences. Seeing within a wholes approach provides a frame for thinking through, as a co-emergent process, actions like raising interest rates, free trade, Sunday shopping, health care user fees, or eliminating rental gardens in High Park. The importance of this mode of thinking is perhaps no more vividly illustrated than in thinking about the environment, where it can be argued that you cannot separate the destruction of the rain forests from the extreme poverty of the populations living in or near the forests, or the grossly skewed consumption patterns of certain industrialized nations.

So I begin here to define, explain, illustrate, and give the significance of a series of basic concepts that come out of a wholes or general systems theory approach. Ideas like "action and inaction are equally causal," and "you can't gauge the ultimate effects of action based on knowledge of input alone" surface as means of framing various current concerns like the feminization of poverty and U.S. militarism in the Persian Gulf.

Though my degree is in sociology and my substantive work has been on issues involved in health and gender, I shall be drawing on examples and illustrations from a wide variety of topics and disciplines. At each turn I shall move through three forms of issues: intimate relations, organizations, and social policy.

PATTERNS IN THEORY

To begin I shall situate a general systems theory approach in the range of types of available theories. This necessitates an inventory of classic approaches and recent advances. The thread I draw through this inventory is looking at how different approaches have brought to light various insights that are uniquely theirs. Since the focus of this book is systems theory, I provide a mere pencil sketch of these theories and leave it to readers to explore some of the excellent available texts that explicate these theories in extensive detail within the social historical contexts of the theorists' lives. At the same time I point out how each of these theories can be advanced by an epistemological shift to a wholes approach via digging out the basic epistemological roots that ultimately handicap conventional theories' applicability and may be invisible because they run so deep.

Social Theory

Conflict theory. Conflict theory has its roots in the work of Karl Marx. The underpinning ideas are assumptions of human benevolence and economic determinism. Taken together these assumptions weave a picture of social life as one where people are pitted against one another in the struggle to get resources. The separation between haves and have-nots, owners and workers, the bourgeoisie and proletariat in the quest for material goods sets these groups in perpetual opposition, or conflict. Marx picked up on Hegel's notion of dialectic, opposing forces, to describe this process and pointed out how this conflict can only be resolved if its basis, capital, was eliminated and ownerships became communal (Wallace & Wolf, 1991). In this manner it would be possible for human beings to act out of respect for others and the community rather than out of self-interest and competition.

The focus of conflict theory is on social structures, or what has been called the macro level. Central notions involve the idea of collective consciousness and means of raising consciousness through making the conclusions of historical comparative analysis known. The works of Marx are debated today in the original. Additionally there has been a vast proliferation of scholarship in the Marxist tradition. Current focus on political economy, structural analysis, and elements of feminist theories attest to the vast influence and permeation of this theory.

Consensus theory. Consensus theory has its roots in a variety of sources, notably Auguste Comte, Emile Durkheim, and Herbert Spencer. Core to this approach is the assumption that human beings are intrinsically greedy and insatiable (Wallace & Wolf, 1991). Social structures that arise do so in a natural progression toward the advance of society and in the necessary containment and direction of insatiable human desires. In this vein society is viewed like a machine or organism where each part contributes in different ways to the maintenance and improvement of the whole. Which person plays which part is sorted out based on natural competition with those most capable taking on the most difficult tasks and being rewarded differentially based on the difficulty of the task and the process of attaining the role. The structure of society is based on consensus that there is basic agreement about what is important. Where conflict does occur it is a minor deviation that does not challenge the wisdom of the whole, or it is a temporary setback in the overall path of progress. Where social problems like alcoholism, crime, or pollution occur, they are predictable slippages in a societal machine that is generally functioning well and in the interest of the common good.

Central notions are (1) nonsummativity—the idea that the whole is greater than the sum of its parts; (2) evolution—the advancement of society through competition; and (3) function—everything serves a function to the system, its existence being evidence of its necessity. The goal of analysis is to seek out universal principles of social functioning so as to fine-tune the social machine and develop the most smoothly running form with the lowest degree of slippage possible. A policy like increasing drunk driving penalties is designed to use fear of punishment to reduce this behavior.

Symbolic interactionism. Symbolic interactionism begins with the idea that human beings are creative or reflexive in their behavior and through this in the ways they mediate their experience. The ability to have symbols, meanings about aspects of life experience, which are shared by the group is the precursor to the existence of language. These symbol sets and their negotiation in varying contexts throughout life in changing circumstances become the focus of analysis. Such symbolic interaction begins the study of what has been called the "micro level," the everyday life of face-to-face interaction in human groups.

A central notion is self—the ability to reflect on one's behavior in concert with others and form an inner dialogue about appropriate and desired behavior that determines which actions are undertaken. The thrust of inquiry is to delve into subjective meanings developed in human groups often by becoming part of the group or observing at close quarters.

The macro/micro debate. Level. Taken together conflict, consensus, and symbolic interaction form the macro/micro debate, the gap between the immediate everyday and subjective and the abstract, societal, and objective. The existence of this gap has drawn a great deal of current attention and was the defining issue for the American Sociological Association's annual meeting in San Francisco in 1989. It is the basis of two schools of thought in terms of which level of analysis is more important, the macro or the micro, the societal or the interpersonal.

Implicit in the debate about level is an underlying notion of causality in the sense that argument over which is more important, the macro or the micro, seems to rest on determining which has greater causal influence. As I shall argue later in greater detail, this can be phrased as a more fundamental problem with conventional reliance on linear causality. Mechanistic models of cause and effect that necessitate separating out variables and apportioning cause are bound to set in motion a debate about which is more causal. Attempts to reconcile or link the macro and micro have fallen back on this underlying epistemology by trying to assign cause, and with it, blame. My feeling is that this has served to widen rather than narrow the gap, particularly since statistical analyses are more often the method of choice for macro-level strategies. This sets up a situation where the means of resolve is skewed from the start toward one position.

Methods. Implicit in this debate is which mode of inquiry is most appropriate, the objective or the subjective. Use of a notion of the macro level necessitates an accompanying notion of society as an abstract. We cannot *see* Canadian society or American social structures. Their existence must be inferred because they exist outside of our immediate experience. Looking for this abstraction outside of humans' experiences means being objective, trying to stay outside of the phenomena. Marx's approach to this was to acknowledge that there is historical specificity to current knowledge, and then to escape this subjectivity by going back in time or across cultures using historical comparative analysis. Consensus theorists such as Durkheim dealt with the issue by staying at arm's length from the data they collected, examining suicide rates for example (Wallace & Wolf, 1991). The goal here is to drill out subjective bias, which may keep research from reaching accurate interpretation.

Contrarily, micro-level analysis takes the stance that what is of interest is that which is subjective and has meaning for the groups being studied. Symbolic interactionists do see their subjects, often spending a great deal of time in interaction with them. W. F. Whyte spent time with street gangs in Chicago (1943/1981), Erving Goffman with mental patients (1961), Joan Emerson with patients undergoing gynecological examinations (1970), and Barbara Hanson with nursing home residents (1985). The goal in each instance was to capture what the subjective experience in each setting was for the persons involved. These subjective experiences are then crafted into sensitizing constructs that try to communicate what it is like to be in any of these settings and why people behave the way they do.

In issues of methods around the macro/micro debate the question of aggregation versus context arises. Though this issue has not gotten the same attention as objectivity versus subjectivity, I feel it may be as, if not more, crucial to sorting out the nature of paradoxes between the macro and micro. It is perhaps less obvious because it revolves around the practicalities of research and therefore its theoretical relevance may have been missed.

In essence this issue involves the determination of what is the unit of analysis and how that unit is sought in the course of research design. In the case of macro-level analysis the unit of interest is the societal or general social property. In order to derive the social structure or property, data are derived from individuals and then aggregated into an estimation of the whole. This would be the case where individuals are surveyed by telephone prior to an election in order to get a feel for the general pattern in the population of voters as a whole. The general is discerned based on the average and this becomes the property.

Contrarily, attention to context means defining units such that it is the particular, rather than the universal, that is of interest. Because meaning is subjective, answers and issues are particular to the meaning group where they originate. To extend the case above, we might discover that while the largest proportion of voters (48%) favor a right wing party, the *majority* of voters (52%) split among indifference or less prevalent alternative parties do not favor that party. Or, while the majority of voters in total support pro-life, the majority of women support pro-choice. Each example presents a different side to the issue of aggregation. First, because aggregation to the universal assumes that the most prevalent is the general, even if not the majority, it means that the most frequent will be taken as general will or consensus. This is of particular relevance if we consider that variance explained by aggregate models rarely exceeds 30 or 40% in the social sciences. This means that the general is deduced, based on assumption of the universal, even when models leave 60 or 70% unexplained.

Second, a majority of an entire population does not take into account the interests of particular groups. Thus, while a majority of members of parliament may vote in favor of a law restricting abortion, if they are primarily white, middle- and upper-class men, they may be voting from a perspective that is more detached from the subjective experience of the women who seek abortions.

In total the issue of retaining particular context versus searching for the general via aggregation highlights how we move from the theoretical to the practical and what it means in terms of interpreting results. Does the average represent the particular? Does perceived statistical predominance represent consensus, or a lowest common denominator, or the views of the most powerful?

Theories of Individual Behavior

Behaviorism. One of the most highly debated theories of this century has been behaviorism. The essential assumption here is the equivalence of humans with other species. The artifacts of humanness are just that, artifacts, with no inherent meaning, deity, morality, dignity, or principle. Humans behave in accordance with how they are trained by a series of rewards and punishments. Deviant or conforming behavior is explained in terms of the modes of rewards and punishments in the environment. B. F. Skinner, who popularized this stance, went on to envision a form of utopian society, *Walden Two* (1948), where the environment is perfected through carefully engineered control. This control would eliminate alleged human traits like envy, embarrassment, greed, and so on, which are at the heart of deviance and competition. In this ideal world there would be no crime or disappointment.

The methods of inquiry involve a strict adherence to logical positivism with strong reliance on the idea of nomotheism, the idea that you can derive universal properties based on the observation of individuals and then aggregating these data into average properties. In behaviorism this is extended to mean that not only can you generalize from the individual to the general, you can generalize from the animal to the human. Vast literatures on the discovery of human intelligence have emerged in this tradition based on laboratory experiments on animals, primarily rodents and to a lesser extent birds and primates. I myself recall checking out a second-year psychology course. I was interested until I found out that for the major assignment I would be "assigned" a rat which I would "shape" (meaning train by reward and punishment) and observe. After the assignment the rat would be destroyed, given that it would then be useless for subsequent research, having been trained.

This anecdote illustrates, in addition to the assumption of human to animal equivalence, the importance of control, or isolation of all possible factors such that a direct relationship between a single cause and observed effect can be inferred. Because of this my rat, had I continued with the course, was useless because once trained, it was not possible to infer a direct causal relationship since it would not be clear whether or not it was my previous training or the next trainer's that was causing subsequent behavior. This stance is directed at maintaining strict objectivity and eliminating all elements of subjectivity, therefore context, from research.

Psychoanalysis. Arguably one of the most pervasive, influential theories of the 20th century, psychoanalysis, like Marxist theory, continues to be debated in its original form, in addition to spawning a profusion of elaborations, extensions, and counter-theories. It begins with the assumption of human subconsciousness. Sigmund Freud posited a tripartite model of human nature: id, ego, and superego. Humans are driven by subconscious desires for life and death (id) that are managed by the emerging ego, which listens to the guilt-evoking superego. The thwarting of desire and accompanying destruction of self-esteem in the course of growing up caused by having sexual, eating, and death impulses judged sick or inappropriate leads to repression of these desires. This repression appears in problems in functioning such as impotence, alcoholism, frigidity, and so on. The task of psychoanalysis is to dig into the unconscious and release pent up frustration and self-disgust by hypnotizing or looking at the dreams of the patient, or analysand.

The principal alliance in method is to a positivist approach stressing the objectivity of the analyst. However, the search for meaning and interpretation in the individual would seem to allow for a model of a creative subjective human.

THEORY OF PATTERNS

A brief review of these major approaches shows an array of assumptions about the nature of humans and what the central features of behavior are. Here is where the potential of a wholes approach shines through, in transforming the conventional assumption-based debates by providing a new language or meta-theory for confronting issues that allows for, but does not necessitate, assumptions. In so doing it provides a pan-disciplinary and a-assumptive theoretical approach that captures new modes of thinking about the world that are not tied to the specifics of cultural, disciplinary, ideological, or political debates. Instead the focus becomes patterned redundancies when observing systems, those sequences of events that repeat and in so doing are amenable to description.

Each conventional theory reviewed is pinned to an assumption (or assumptions), something which is taken as true. Specific derivatives like Marx's dialectic or Freud's id flow from an initial stance on what is believed to be true, such as human benevolence or subconscious. This is the conventional mode for theory. Begin with an assumption, derive and test ideas that follow. Because of this, this type of theory is tied to its assumptions. Any challenge or advance of this type of theory is ultimately bounded by the assumptions in question. Thus, critique cannot go beyond this. You either accept the assumption or do not.

Acceptance of the assumptions may be tied to any number of motivations: religious, political, emotional, or ideological. However, because acceptance is belief-based there is no chance of resolve. There is an impasse because the ideas form a paradox—ideas true individually that cannot be true together. The Marxist assumption of intrinsic human benevolence is irreconcilable with Durkheim's assumption of intrinsic human greed. By way of analogy the pro-life/pro-choice debate shows up the same principle. Inherent in the sides' names are the bases of the debate. One side sees abortion as a question of murder, the other as a question of control over one's body. In both the case of the theorists and that of the abortion debaters, there is no hope for resolve because their positions are grounded in totally irreconcilable assumptions about what is the true nature of the issue. Thus, the process of argument leading to advance, reminiscent of Hegel's notion of dialectic, is precluded. Instead there remains a kind of "my mom's better that your mom" pattern with resolve coming only in terms of which side is more numerous or has the power to enforce its will.

This is where a wholes or general systems theory approach promises to transcend the classic debates, by freeing theoretical debate from assumptive paradox. Instead of beginning with an assumption, it begins instead with a point of departure, nonsummativity, which states that the whole is greater than the sum of its parts. This idea invites analysis of varying kinds to begin wherever it seems relevant, wherever there is some phenomena that exhibits properties when two or more parts are put together that are not present in those parts alone. Though systems approaches have been used to a variety of ends with a variety of assumptions, I take the stance here that this single point of departure is the sole requisite of a wholes approach. Any of the elements that I, or others, add to it are options.

This difference in basic structure sets up general systems theory as an approach rather than a theory in the conventional form. In essence a systems or wholes approach is targeted at a new way of seeing the world for purposes of understanding it. In this manner it challenges and transcends more conventional approaches by providing an alternative to a mechanistic way of viewing the world that underpins all of the theories I reviewed. Each of the theories is trapped by debates about determinacy framed as a question of level, by a model of linear causality, or by a mechanistic approach to units. By suggesting alternatives in contexts, cybernetic causality, and relational units, a systems approach is able to reform conventional theories while leaving their inherent assumptions intact. This provides a means of advance within the confines of each theory, while at the same time allowing for a language that is shared across theories. A Marxist approach can benefit from use of the language of equifinality to describe the inevitability of conflict. Parallels can be found in the high rates of recidivism in spousal violence, which may be examined by a behaviorist.

In sum, a wholes approach provides a means of reframing the classical debates about assumptions to which conventional theories are tied. This lies in an epistemological shift to seeing a world of relational wholes, rather than discrete individual pieces. The power of this shift in seeing is witnessed when we stop to consider how the history of the 20th century has pointed increasingly in the direction of issues that are relational to the extent of being global in nature. Perhaps the most significant event in this direction was the development and deployment of the first atomic bomb.

The earliest thinkers of the systems approach, Wiener and Rosenbluth, began articulating the concept of cybernetics in the A-bomb's aftermath and reflect a self-conscious science informed by the new revelation that science does not operate in a vacuum. A thought can ultimately lead to mass destruction. Einstein's equation $E = mc^2$ led in multifinal fashion to the destruction of Hiroshima and Nagasaki. Recognition of the role of science and the need for a socially conscious science is reflected in N. Wiener's book *Cybernetics* (1948).

This development in the physical sciences was echoed in the close link between general systems theory and the rise of peace and conflict studies, exemplified by the work of Rapoport (1974). In the escalation of the arms race, the Vietnam War, and more recently the Gulf War, the appropriateness of a wholes approach came to prominence. The zero sum game as a metaphor for global armed conflict became a question of central attention. Here Rapoport points out vividly how the need for a wholes conception of inquiry is demonstrated by the move toward wars. ". . . [T]he First World War was the chemists' war: high explosives and poison gas were the gifts of chemistry. The Second World War owes its achievements to the physicists, who gave us radar and the atomic bomb. The Third World War is seen by those who are planning it as a mathematician's war, the war of computers and guided missiles" (Rapoport, 1989, p. 160). This mode of war planning is shown in the 1983 movie *War Games*, where probabilities for success by one side and the costs in casualties are constantly assessed by a computer.

What a wholes approach points out in this instance is that there is no such thing as a discrete war, in the sense of direct cause and effect, win and lose. Seeing the issue in terms of winners and losers leads to a false notion that the effects of war are containable, predictable, finite. In order to make this point clear and advocate a safe deterrent to war, peace and conflict theorists developed the concept of nuclear winter. Through calculation they demonstrated that any thermonuclear war, in addition to immediate damage in terms of loss of life and destruction, would send the world into a quasi-glacier age. The fires created by bombing would produce such a mass of smoke and related contaminants that the atmosphere would no longer allow sunlight to pass, setting the planet into a perpetual winter. This multifinal outcome, nuclear winter, presented a possible deterrent to nuclear war by stockpiling highly combustible materials next to prime targets for bombing, such as military installations (Rapoport, 1989). The relevance of a wholes approach here is to point out how looking beyond initial causes and effects toward ongoing patterns of feedback suggests a new means of seeing the debate.

The importance of a systems approach can be seen in the attempts to frame the Gulf War as "containable" based on using conventional weapons, a simple case of removing a threat by blasting it away. The war was undertaken without thinking through how this supposedly discrete action would magnify in the global system. Has it ultimately strengthened Saddam Hussein's position? What will be the ultimate effects of hundreds of thousands of civilians being killed during the war, referred to as "collateral damage," borrowing the metaphor of medicine? I wrote the first draft of this text in the spring of 1992. The importance of looking at long-term events became clear to me when the U.S. military forces were again dispatched to the Persian Gulf in August 1992, co-emergent with the 1992 presidential campaign. In 1994, George Bush was ousted, while Saddam Hussein remained in power.

There are three elements of a systems approach that promise to transcend the kind of linear, mechanistic, short-term epistemology that led to embarking on the Gulf War: cybernetics, relational units, and process.

In terms of linearity, the systems alternative to causality is to look away from simple finite causal sequences and look instead to the cybernetic, self-steering nature of systems of two or more parts. In this manner it is possible to frame the Gulf War as a result of an ongoing feedback process that maintains the war industry in the U.S. When the Cold War began to thaw the industry that fueled it remained, meaning that a new enemy threat would co-emerge in order to maintain the seesaw pattern of escalation, advance, and immediate obsolescence of weaponry. It is possible to see past the dichotomy of level in that assigning cause or determinacy to any one part, level or otherwise, becomes moot. It is the co-emergent concert production that becomes relevant rather than attempts to assign cause, and with it blame, either wholly or partially.

Seeing the relational as opposed to the mechanistic means seeing *defense* itself as a relational term. There is no defense without two or more parts; it is a pattern that co-emerges between parts and is not seen in either part alone. Threats, perceived or otherwise, can only exist with two or more parties playing in concert to create and maintain the notion.

Long-term thinking is a metaphor for shifting from seeing phenomena as ending to seeing them as ongoing processes. This is a subtle distinction in that we may believe that we are thinking in process terms but in practice we are thinking in finite pieces of a process by virtue of the way we divide up phenomena to study them. By overlaying a linear cause and effect model on a process, we imply that effects are finite without considering their interactive continuity. Consider the initial effects of something like the proposed fixed link between New Brunswick and Prince Edward Island (PEI). The short-term benefit was phrased as job creation. However, in the long run the effects of the fixed link cannot be predicted based just on the initial effect. What, for example, will happen to the agricultural base of the PEI economy if middle- and upper-class people begin buying up farmland for luxury homes and commute to Halifax?

Another example of problems in thinking in terms of single linear cause and effect versus interactional ongoing process is the case of ballet training. Insisting on skeletal proportions for female dancers may set off a lifelong pattern of anorexia and bulimia, drug use, or chronic injury. Or, insisting on training techniques that change bone structure before it is fully formed may force age limitations on the career of a dancer. These dynamics are chronicled in Gelsey Kirkland's autobiography *Dancing on My Grave* (1986).

In each instance a wholes approach means seeing not just the initial effects but how these effects are reacted to, how the process amplifies and mutates from the original. Within a wholes approach the concepts of feedback, equifinality and multifinality can be used to talk about these patterns in systems.

A wholes or general systems theory approach surfaces as a language for describing patterns in phenomena of interest, using nonsummativity (the whole is greater than the sum of its parts) as a point of departure. It is in essence a theory of patterns that allows for articulating a series of concepts that work on a new form of epistemological stance, seeing the world in terms of wholes.

ORGANIZATION

This book is in two nonsummative parts leading to a co-emergent wholes approach. Part One sets up some basics of a general systems theory approach, which are derived from a host of disciplines in the physical and social sciences, and are relevant to any system of two or more interrelated parts. Part Two adds a number of ideas that other authors and I have developed in order to analyze human systems, and that may have relevance for other kinds of systems.

For simplicity I have divided the book into a number of subsections. Each presents one idea, shown initially under the heading, then developed in detail. In these sections, I define, explain, and illustrate on the levels of intimacy, organization, and social policy, give derivations and extensions, and conclude with the significance. In this manner there will be repetitive patterns for readers to follow as we greet an array of ideas.

PART ONE

CONCEPTS

*Concepts are ideas, often abstractions, which are developed in
order to explain something such that you can move from
the particular to the general.*

The move to create concepts is a move from a specific observation to an idea or
principle that applies beyond the single instance. Take a simple example:

See Spot Run. See Jane run.
See Spot and Jane run together.
Spot and Jane appear to have a relationship.
This is an example of a mutually satisfying relationship.
Animal caretaker relationships are an example of the concept of positive
feedback.

As the observations go on, in each instance we are moving away from a
specific observation and toward a more general principle that can be transported
to other situations in order to aid in understanding. While Spot and Jane demonstrate positive feedback, a situation where together they make each other hap-
pier, this is not the only type of positive feedback. Positive feedback is any
feedback that leads to change. Thus, becoming sadder would be positive feedback as well, as would be escalating unemployment. The concept that began
with Spot and Jane has application to many other phenomena. This means developing concepts, as opposed to discrete observations, allows a common ground
or language for talking about a variety of issues and allows analysts to transport
insights developed in one instance to others.

Concepts in the realm of intimacy could be equality versus inequality, situations where persons in an intimate relationship share tasks and resources such
that both contribute and benefit equally or, conversely, where one partner gives

more than he or she gets. In an organization a concept like resource allocation can be developed to capture a wide range of resources beyond what the simpler category of money may capture. Pure monetary cost-benefit models may be less relevant than those that take into account issues such as job satisfaction, burn-out, feeling of involvement, or perceived worth to the organization. For instance the concept of asymmetry reflects a situation where sides are not equally balanced. This is often seen in architecture, fashion, or art, with Victorian houses that have a flat facade with windows on one side and a round porch on the other, a woman's dress with one shoulder bare, or Picasso's portraits with more parts on one side than the other. In social policy this has been used to describe a situation where the particular rights of constituencies like the handicapped, aboriginal peoples, and women are protected by giving these groups equal participation. An abstract concept provides a means of framing or talking about issues that allows a means of transcending and thus advancing the particular.

Concept making becomes a key step in moving forward because it shows a way out of what may be irreconcilable debates. Allocating decision-making votes based on the model of parliamentary representation or simple majority would mean that constituencies such as aboriginal peoples, the handicapped, or women would not have a voice in their destiny.

A concept like asymmetry gives an alternative form for representation, one which is based on particular needs and rights, rather than simple numeric representation. This gives form and a principle that can be written into law. For instance, it underpins the rationale for the allocation of wheelchair parking and universal access to facilities. Even though persons in wheelchairs may not comprise a majority of voters, the principle of asymmetry would mean that their particular needs and rights should be respected.

Concepts underpin various political debates about renaming, and in so doing transforming, various categories or behaviors. The significance of concepts in social policy is seen in the change of the term "rape" to "sexual assault." Underlying this change is the notion that this is an act of violence rather than passion or sexual exploration. This change of concept, along with its connotations, has implications all down the line for reporting, charging, prosecuting, defending, rendering verdicts, sentencing, and determining parole. Another example, as will be discussed in various places in this book, was the renaming of GRIDS (Gay Related Immune Deficiency Syndrome) to AIDS (Acquired Immune Deficiency Syndrome).

The significance of concepts for theory is in terms of their being the currency of theoretical development and advance. Concepts allow theorists to talk to one another, exchange ideas and learn by applying the same concepts to different substantive issues. Research is driven by a search for developing, testing and refining concepts. Research is a process of going from concepts to measurement, then data collection, analysis, and refinement of concepts. Conceptualization is thus a central goal in the theorizing and research process.

Understanding of a somewhat abstract theoretical approach such as the one I present in this book can be facilitated through the use of concepts. They give a way of talking about or framing everyday experiences and issues of concern. Pressing problems like environmental degradation, racism, sexism, crime, homelessness, starvation and undernourishment, are creeping into the experience of the general population. Work on these problems can be guided by first looking at what concepts have brought them to the surface, then rethinking concepts in order to solve the problems.

For example, the belief that Western civilizations and the middle class are somehow insulated from the effects of these problems can be framed as summativity: problems can be isolated to parts of a system. Modes of summative, isolationist thinking may have led in multifinal fashion to problems, once exotic and the turf of the academic or politician, which are now the stuff of everyday experience in all sectors of the population and regions of the planet. Pollution and ultraviolet rays are becoming more difficult to avoid or escape, even if you can afford to try. Poverty is becoming a viable threat to the middle class, especially to women and parents. Rethinking these issues in a nonsummative view unearths the co-emergent nature of these problems and allows us to see how sexism and racism in industrialized nations lead in equifinal fashion to escalating global pollution and poverty.

What this suggests is that theory, as presented here, is something that needs to permeate into the public consciousness as a means of challenging the conventional modes of analysis, not just the conclusions derived. This means questioning not just the "whats" of seeing but also the "hows" of viewing as a means of critique and reform through a wholes approach.

Chapter 2

Context

*Contexts are emergent wholes in groups of two
or more interrelated parts.*

Apparently one day Konrad Lorenz, a famous scholar who did extensive work around the nature–nurture debate, was in his yard conducting an experiment. He was testing how ducks learn. In order to do this he was trying to teach the baby ducks how to quack and flap their wings. He went around the yard quacking and flapping and eventually encouraged the little ducks to do likewise. Imagine how this scene appeared to his neighbors (Watzlawick, Beavin, & Jackson, 1967).

A researcher was talking to a patient in a psychiatric hospital, who when asked what his problem was said that he was a "tennis ball." The researcher thought this pathological and decided to look deeper. He asked to be invited to dinner with the patient and his parents. At the dinner table he began to observe a process whereby the son was seated between the parents who began a series of discussions and arguments directed at each other but directed through the son. They sent missives and criticisms at one another using the son as the carrier, often the stated cause of the problem. After watching this process for some time, it became clear that what appeared as very pathological, referring to oneself as a tennis ball, was in fact a metaphor for the way the patient felt in his intimate relationships.

While I was doing work in nursing homes I came to know one resident of the home, Scarlett. She was the most outwardly disturbed and difficult of all the residents in the home. She said she was Mrs. Houdini, was constantly agitated, fought with staff, and ran or walked all day long if not in restraints. Had her financial status not permitted her a personal full-time aide in addition to the home's staff, she would have been in a higher level care setting and would likely have been under sedation or physical restraint. As the activity director, I arranged a wine and cheese party for the residents. Imagine my surprise when Scarlett arrived dressed immaculately a few minutes early without an aide, and offered to help with the party. She corrected my arrangements where things were placed on the wrong side or where I had the wrong wine-with-cheese combinations. She helped serve at the party; knew all the residents by name; and even shared jokes, inferences, and confidences with others as she continued at the party. I was dumbfounded. How could this person who was so obviously disturbed at other times and who had been diagnosed as such, be so connected, wise, and ostensibly normal in this setting? It was my confusion that drew me back into academia and ultimately led me to ground my thinking centrally in the notion of context.

As each of the above stories illustrates in different ways, it is very difficult to understand behavior outside its context, and problems emerge when we do not share context. Without knowing Lorenz's scholarly work, would we think him anything but crazy? Ditto seeing the "tennis ball's" parents or Scarlett's behavior in the nursing home. Behaviors are embedded in inextricably linked contexts, such that their particular nature may be knowable only within their native context.

Imagine for a moment two houses on the same street, the same behavior in each, a spouse cooking bacon. Upon smelling the bacon, the other spouse at 201 thinks, "She's trying to apologize, that's sweet," while at 203, the thought is, "What's he trying to do, turn me into a blimp so I'm trapped with him?" Each reaction to the same stimulus requires knowledge of the patterns in the relationship, its context, before its effect and meaning can be understood or decoded. Imagine the boardroom of a fast food chain where they are trying to decide how to expand their menu. When they tried introducing muffins in the U.K. it was a total flop, but in North America it was a major success. Why? Luckily the newest member of the board did her graduate work in London. "Muffins are not something with which the English people are familiar. Have you considered adding cakes instead, particularly in cricket season?"

In the TV Ontario Sociology Series on Sociology, Susan McDaniel discussed why attempts to spread birth control knowledge and equipment have succeeded in reducing fertility, but only in the middle class of industrialized nations. In developing nations the birth rate remains high (Ontario Educational Communications, 1985). Finally, context sensitive considerations of the contradictions of how child birth is constructed unearthed the idea that while children are a financial drain to the middle class in an industrialized nation, they are a financial asset in impoverished populations. Birth control will be completely ineffective in lowering birth rates if people have no desire to limit family size. Lowering fertility in poverty-stricken populations means raising standards of living.

The origins for the concept of context can be found in a number of places, but the major connection in terms of a general systems theory approach is the concept of nonsummativity (the whole is greater than the sum of its parts), which began with Aristotle (Checkland, 1983) and will be elaborated in detail in the next section of this chapter. The wholes that emerge when two or more parts are interrelated are, in effect, context. The idea of the need to contextualize, or look for relational patterns that are not witnessed in individual parts, runs through a variety of lines of thinking. In psychology, notable examples are Gestalt and field theory (Lewin, 1951). In sociology, strains of structural functionalism, as elaborated by Durkheim or Parsons, make use of the notion of nonsummativity. The Marxist notion of the historical specificity of knowledge echoes the need to interpret in context. Symbolic interaction is founded on notions of subjective shared group meanings that are tied to the nature of the group in question.

Context is significant for theory as a construct that introduces the idea that the target of analysis can be legitimately thought of as wholes, contexts, or relationships, rather than the more common reliance on theory that is designed to dissect phenomena into parts for purposes of analysis. In a metatheoretical sense this provides a leap to a new mode of theory construction that is less prescriptive in terms of the range of phenomena that can be considered.

In terms of research the importance is primarily a challenge to replace conventional practices that require taking apart a phenomena in order to study it. Reliance on statistical procedures to reconstitute a subject is wholly inappropriate. Context is founded in the idea that the whole is more than the sum of its parts, so how can we legitimately try to find wholes by summing parts? Regardless of the complexity or sophistication of procedures (such as structural equation models), when the phenomenon must be divided into discrete pieces either for data collection or data analysis, it cannot approximate wholes. The directive here is to rethink methods in order to retain wholes in all phases of a research design.

The everyday significance lies in beginning to see all our actions in context, in concert, in relationship, with others. Thinking in terms of context means constantly aligning one's actions and inactions with those of others and gauging what events will emerge in the process. Take the example of polling. Has your refusal to answer a questionnaire in a shopping mall or on the phone led to the compiling of data on the silent majority who are assumed to agree? By recycling your bottles, cans, and newspapers are you aiding in the reduction of garbage? Can your current trepidation at returning to college after 15 years away be traced to a pattern of isolation and conditional love during your adolescence?

Context is thus the beginning point for all that is to follow in this book. For me it is the single most significant idea in the wholes approach, thus my choice of the term "wholes" as the cornerstone concept for the book. Wholes is for me a more accessible, less off-putting expression of the notion of context, looking for wholes that emerge with two or more interrelated parts. I have found in the past that a wholes approach is something that people tend to have an intuitive feel for, but their conventional training prevents them from seeing in contextual terms. Once people begin to "unlearn" the strictures of conventional theory and science, a new way of seeing things emerges that helps to capture things that remained just outside of the grip of conventional viewing lenses. The power and the mystery of this type of viewing stance is somewhat like the shift Alice made when she stepped through the looking glass. Previous learning is suspended in order to explore things that were hidden by conventional blinders.

> Then she began looking about, and noticed that what could be seen from the old room was quite common and uninteresting, but that all the rest was as different as possible. For instance, the pictures on the wall next to the fire seemed to be all alive, and the very clock on the chimney-piece (you know you can only see the back of it in the Looking-glass) had got the face of a little old man, and grinned at her. (Carroll, 1865/1981, p. 11)

This struck me as a fitting analogy to the kind of viewing stance a wholes approach sets up and the way things begin to appear that were taken for granted before, but now seem different and worthy of attention. The everyday and commonplace becomes problematic (Smith, 1987) when our means for rendering order on experience is altered.

Within the umbrella concept of context it is possible to determine three more specific concepts: nonsummativity, system, and unit. I shall go through each in turn below. In so doing I concretize the basic orientation of context and link my descriptions to the broader writings of general systems theory that cross a variety of disciplines in the social, physical, and natural sciences.

NONSUMMATIVITY

The whole is greater than the sum of its parts.

Humpty Dumpty sat on a wall:
Humpty Dumpty had a great fall.
All the King's Horses and all the King's men
Couldn't put Humpty Dumpty in his place again. (Carroll, 1946)

Both of the above suggest the same thing. There are things that emerge only together and therefore cannot be taken apart and put back together. This idea, referred to as nonsummativity is, at its most basic, the notion that the whole is greater than the sum of its parts. It points out that things emerge when two parts act together that are not seen in those parts alone. This idea challenges the strategy of trying to figure out the world by taking it apart into components such as variables and then adding those parts up to get a picture of the phenomena. Doing so would be like trying to unscramble eggs, or put Humpty Dumpty back together again.

With nonsummativity is implied the idea that because emergent wholes are features of the relationship, rather than the individual, relational patterns in human systems may not be known to the individual. This in itself may explain how intervention into human group systems became so closely tied with the elaboration of systems theory in the behavioral sciences and gave rise to family therapy. The therapeutic task can begin with the notion of nonsummativity as a guideline to finding, and perhaps pointing out to clients, those patterns in relationships of which the members are unaware but which seem to be at the heart of specific individual behaviors such as anorexia, abuse, incest, or failure at school.

In essence the abstract principle that the whole is greater than the sum of its parts directs attention to emergent relational wholes, looking for patterns that exist between, rather then within, individuals. This means constantly aligning any observation or insight about a part with how it fits the whole, or context. You cannot understand the rise in prostitution in Toronto without looking at changes in antiprostitution laws in New York State. A child's obesity must be interpreted in terms of a context of conditional love. The killing of elephants for ivory by local populations needs to be framed in the extreme poverty of the country where the proceeds from a single tusk may be many times the annual income for a family. In each instance a single behavior needs to be related to the context, or the patterns of emergent wholes, to which it is tied.

One of my favorite examples for nonsummativity is the television show *The Newlywed Game*, where couples are asked questions separately about what their spouse would say. The game becomes interesting relative to nonsummativity when the spouses are put back together and the spouse who answered first waits with his or her answers on cards on his or her lap. The other spouse is then asked the same question. Often the responses evoke anger, shock, even violence—hitting with the answer cards or hands. Quite frequently one spouse retracts an answer. "No, no, you're right, honey." This shows up quite vividly how the whole is greater than the sum of its parts in that we see directly a situation where parts are separated then put back together. The discrete parts are less telling than how those parts, in this case individual responses, are contextualized by the whole. When there is discrepancy, whose will prevails, and whose is dismissed? What kind of pattern typifies relationships that lead to violence? These are nonsummative kinds of questions, those which focus on emergent patterns in the relationship and read any single behavior event only in terms of how it fits patterns in a context.

On an organizational level, I am constantly interested in decision making in groups, be it a committee or an informal context. One particular example is my experience with groups of people attending conferences who have decided to go out to dinner together and are in the process of deciding on a restaurant. These groups tend to be very mixed, with some people knowing each other well and for a long time and others joining based on a brief acquaintance. I recall one particular time when a couple of suggestions for nearby restaurants with standard fare (pasta, meat, continental) were put forth. After some discussion it was decided that we would go to a restaurant that was expensive, would require a 45-minute taxi ride, and served only beer, along with a highly specialized menu of primarily spicy dishes. The meal was dreadful, expensive, and slow. On later talking with others in the group they shared my dismay at how we ended up going to such a place when there were several inexpensive wide variety places within walking distance.

I offer no explanation for how this decision emerged out of a context where individually the large majority of members were opposed to it. It is an example of how nonsummative wholes emerge separate from parts, even where the sum of those parts are contrary to the emergent decision. The context-sensitive directive would be to look at how this pattern repeated. Did the same phenomenon emerge when deciding on a restaurant among all groups at the conference, or only with the sociologists? In so doing it would be possible to look for patterns and begin explanation.

In terms of social policy the importance of nonsummativity can be illustrated by events in South Africa where the majority of the population was opposed to racial segregation, yet in total this majority did not explain the nonsummative whole of continued apartheid. As free democratic elections approached in 1994, violence erupted between the ANC party, which was expected to win the election, and the opposing Zulus. Political and social policy decisions are replete with examples where pure sum questions, what proportion of voters are in favor or against, do not predict the nonsummative wholes that emerge.

Nonsummativity can be traced as far back as Aristotle (Checkland, 1983; von Bertalanffy, 1975) and has since run through a variety of lines of thought. It is a basic principle of the structural functionalist school of thinking in sociology. Durkheim echoed the concept of nonsummativity in his justification of the idea that since there are emergent wholes in society that are outside the individuals who make up these wholes, they can be thought of as external to human experience. This was the jumping board for studying human group processes as external, calling for an objective mode of inquiry of these "social facts" that could be studied in the same manner as other external phenomena like tidal waves and birds (Ashley & Orenstein, 1990). Parsons and Merton later made use of this concept to outline a model of society somewhat like a machine or organism with parts contributing to the whole in known or unknown fashion (Wallace & Wolf, 1991). The principle of emergence as a theoretical construct came to be used by them to justify a notion that the structure of society is based on consensus, in that it was merely emergent rather than imposed or controlled as would be envisioned by Marx. Things exist because they are functional and serve a purpose to the society even if that purpose is not immediately known or appears destructive to certain parts of society. Nonsummativity is *de rigueur* to systems approaches that underpin analysis of family systems as focused on in therapy. Notable in this tradition are the works of Bateson et al. (1956), Watzlawick et al. (1967), Lidz (1957) and Wynne, Rycoff, Day, and Hirsh (1958). Here the use of nonsummativity is different than in the functionalist setting. Looking at relationships as wholes spawns a number of constructs that can be used to understand sustained patterns that manifest into symptoms of mental illness in a family member. Thus a basic notion of pathology rather than health pervades. Considering these two different stances together reiterates a central theme for this book: it is the assumptions of a particular analyst, not a general systems theory approach, which justify any prescriptive conclusions in ideological, social, or political terms. The status quo, conservative, sometimes reactionary bent of a functionalist approach is as true and untrue as the critical stance of the therapist. By way of analogy Cristian Barnard and Jack the Ripper both used knives to gain fame. It is, however, not the knife that determined either the form of their actions or their fame. A wholes approach, like some knives with a number of attachments, is a tool that does not determine how it or the attachments are used.

I have extended the notion of nonsummativity in my own work on intimate relations to look at how emergent wholes are relevant to the development of mental illness in general and senile dementia in particular (Hanson, 1989a). In this article I examine how a specific construction, the idea that something is wrong with someone, emerges and is maintained. Specifically, I spotted an emotional pattern whereby there is isolation of one individual such that they are not privy to shifts of constructed realities. Because of this, the isolated person is constantly considered wrong or crazy. Watching for the correlating patterns in nonsummative contexts of intimacy showed me that it was not that the person considered sick *did not* know what was real, rather they *could not* know what was real. I add another form of application of the basic principle of nonsummativity, by linking it to notions of constructivism or subjective meaning that run through radical constructivism (von Glasersfeld, 1984), symbolic interactionism (Blumer, 1969), and post-modernism (Murphy, 1988). It presents a different type of extension of a wholes or general systems theory approach to different conclusions, given that the assumptions I write on the principle of nonsummativity are different.

Nonsummativity is significant to theory as it presents an alternative point of departure both in terms of structure of theory and content. By beginning with a point of departure rather than a prescriptive assumption or assumptions, a wholes approach to theory is at once more flexible within a discipline or topic and more amenable to a greater range of disciplines and topics. In terms of content, by promoting an epistemological shift to seeing the world in terms of relational wholes, it is an alternative to more reductionist or mechanical models that encourage study through dissection, then reconstitution, as is traditional in classical biology and medicine. Beginning with and retaining wholes means seeing phenomena in complex flowing relational wholes, necessitating shifts in thinking and practice like moving into a natural setting, as opposed to working in a laboratory, to conduct the observation of a species. Or in medicine the permeation of a systems approach can be seen in holistic medicine, lifestyle medicine, and diagnostics like barium tests and angiograms, which allow watching the body in motion, its parts in concert.

Reform of research statistics is perhaps the most challenging notion. By definition the mathematics that underpin statistics are summative. Reforming statistics means going to forms of mathematics that can capture nonsummative wholes. Collection of data needs to be approached such that relationships are the central focus and are retained intact throughout a research design from conception, through collection of data and on to analysis and conclusion. In the case of intimate relationships as illustrated by *The Newlywed Game* couples, this would mean collecting data on couples as wholes, rather than as individuals whose data is summed into wholes. An interesting twist here would be reintroducing individually derived data back into the nonsummative context, as is in fact done in the TV show. Here the opportunity to see the importance of seeing wholes as opposed to parts in isolation is made clear. It also provides an additional form of data to use in spotting patterns, in that it is a form of experimentation or "poking" the phenomena to see how it reacts. Everyday relevance may be found by being aware of how emergent nonsummative wholes are set in motion. Perhaps knowledge of the process in groups, small or large, can give individuals a means of resisting the imposition of the will of the few upon the many.

SYSTEM

A system can be defined as any two or more parts that are related,
such that change in any one part changes all parts.

This focuses on any part and any interrelation in situations where change in one part changes all parts. It is the basis of systemic, or ecological, thinking. The central connection here is that if parts form a system (are interconnected), there is no such thing as a single cause and effect relationship. Any action or inaction will reverberate through the entire system leading to unpredictable effects and sometimes effects that are precisely the inverse of the intended effect.

One of the more tragic examples of the principle of system, interconnected parts where changing one changes all, is the long-term effects of DDT. This was a pesticide designed to kill bugs, which it did. However, because it remained in the systems of bugs, while not directly harming the birds who ate them, it led to softened shells in the birds' eggs. Several species of bug-eating birds were dying off, therefore eating less bugs. So the bugs increased. DDT was eventually banned, but the long-term systemic effects are not fully known. It may have wandered into various forms of plant and animal life, including human foods, through the water system, showing up in concentrations around the Great Lakes watershed (Pim, 1981).

The power of a notion of interconnectedness leading to change in all parts by changing one can be illustrated by moving through several levels of examples. In the field of intimacy I refer to the work of Marshall and Neil (1977). This project chronicles the effects of changing one part of intimate systems, the woman's weight. Through intestinal reduction, a number of married women, underwent drastic and sudden reduction of their body weight. These women were severely overweight before the operation and had been so at the time their spousal relationships were formed. There were a variety of changes in the intimate relationships, including the man being threatened and fearful that his wife would now seek other men, and in some cases sexual interest increased while in others it disappeared. In sum, this example points out how ostensibly simple (in the sense of finite) intervention is in fact complex when entered into a system of interrelated parts.

Imagine the process that occurs when the owner of a business appoints his or her child vice president and names the child as successor. The current board of directors feels threatened by the presence of the child and so begins a process of undercutting his or her skills and performance, and sabotaging his or her work. The parent begins to take credit for all of the child's successes yet every failure or mistake is the child's fault alone. The child becomes depressed, has downward spiralling self-esteem, and begins using drugs to try and cope with the untenable demands. The extended family relations begin to become competitive and hostile as other siblings resent that the heir apparent has been chosen rather than one of them. The chosen is being chased and attacked from every direction and finally snaps, tries to commit suicide, and then withdraws from the family business. Competition between the other siblings and the board of directors intensifies, such that work is not being done because the focus is primarily to enhance an individual position in relation to another. Attempts to sabotage the work of others are frequent. Eventually the business is made fragile and goes into bankruptcy early in the recession. The extended family begins a process of blaming each other for the failure and atomizes. Everything is related to everything.

A recent example of a Nova Scotia fisherman who netted $500,000 worth of bluefin tuna ("Fisherman hits jackpot," 1994) brought home to me the principle that everything is related to everything in international policy. This fisherman happened to net 47 bluefin tuna, which are valued as high as $122 per pound in the Japanese market where they are highly valued for sushi. That's about $10,000 per fish. The relative value of the fish to the fisherman would not be so high if he were not living in the depressed and fragile economy of Atlantic Canada. This pricing is related both to the Japanese preferred foods as well as their burgeoning economic power and relative standing in the world. It is also related to highly successful Japanese management techniques and the banning of armaments in Japan following World War II. Mapping these interconnections could go on indefinitely. The bluefin tuna that will be turned into sushi are part of a global system where everything is related to everything.

Social policy, in this case the combination of local, national, and international policy, has shown some interesting illustrations of the systems principle. The growth of New York City was accompanied by soaring real estate costs within the city, prompting greater buildup of both commercial and residential development in New York State, New Jersey, and Connecticut. How-ever, people living and doing business outside the city and paying taxes to those localities still used the services of New York City. Thus, demand on city services increased while its tax base eroded, leading to major budgetary crises. A systems view here means seeing that you cannot separate what actions such as buildup outside New York City will ultimately mean within the city.

Although developed later and at a less accelerated rate, the city of Toronto has apparently failed to learn from New York City's experience. Built in the second half of the 1900s, the 401 Highway across the northern perimeter of Toronto was designed to speed travel across and into the city. Once this roadway was built, commuting by car became easier, faster, and less expensive, making it possible for residential developments to be started in what was previously farm or natural lands. Since that time the population growth of the Toronto area has led to incorporation of the cities of Mississauga, Vaughn, Markham, Scarborough, and Pickering, which border what was Toronto in the 1960s. As residential developments increased in these cities, the 401 became increasingly crowded. It was therefore expanded along with the creation or expansion of other highways in the region, thus opening up the commutable distance to the center of Toronto. On a recent trip to the east coast of Canada, I noted that after I had passed Yonge Street (often considered to be the central street of Toronto), I drove for one hour on the 401 at highway speeds before I past subdivisions and entered farm and natural land. This example illustrates how a single action changes the whole system. By opening up one intake to Toronto, the effective boundaries of the city have been extended as much as 60 miles in every direction except south across the lake. Even this has been discussed, however, in terms of putting tunnels in the lake, landfilling over the tunnels, and developing over top.

Extended to the international realm, the recent emergence of free trade agreements and trading blocks shows vividly the interconnectedness of parts of systems. The emergence of the EEC (European Economic Community) was at least part of the impetus for the North American Free Trade Act (NAFTA). Recognition of the need for bigger trading blocks and cheaper labor forces fueled the U.S. entry into the broader process of globalism.

In each of these examples a single point emerges: changing one part changes all. This is the essence of a notion of system. By way of metaphor we can think of the process of acting on a system as being somewhat like pushing on a waterbed. Pushing on one corner leads to disruption in all areas, and possibly ultimately back onto the first corner we push. So it is with systems of any kind. If a phenomena demonstrates the principle of systems, being interrelated such that change in one part changes all, then its analysis must be grounded in this central model.

The relevance of a systems concept was perhaps most obvious in the realm of the biological. History is replete with examples where human intervention, either by action or inaction, has had multitudes of effects all the way down the line of the ecology. The Canadian province of Prince Edward Island presents several examples (Blakeley & Vernon, 1963). Until the island was settled by Europeans, there were no mice. Once introduced to the island via ships, mice multiplied vastly to the point that a city was named "Souris" (French for mouse) and retains this name. Contrarily, "Seacow Pond," named for the proliferation of walrus, is a ghostly reminder of the wholesale slaughter of this species during the course of settling the area. The settling of the western U.S. brought the buffalo to the verge of extinction. High demand for ivory outside Africa has led to the near extinction of the elephants within the continent.

A systems notion permeated thinking in the same vein on a more global level when the threat of thermonuclear war surfaced with the invention of the atomic bomb and was fueled by the U.S.–Soviet Union Cold War. I heard Anatol Rapoport speak on the issue at the University of Toronto during the Gulf War in 1991. He pointed out that the Cold War was co-emergent with the massive war industry in the U.S. This industry, which consumes a large proportion of the federal budget, was not about to disappear simply because it became unnecessary when the Cold War began to thaw. So the concept of a "tidy" war emerged. As will be discussed later in greater detail, Saddam Hussein became the new threat and the industry went into high gear. Now the war machine will have the advantage of being able to label its weapons as "combat-tested" at subsequent marketing fairs.

The systems view here is that there is no such thing as a tidy war, in the sense of a war that is confined to conventional weaponry. Even though nuclear weapons were not used in the Gulf War, how much nuclear power generation led to how much residue in the environment, and potential weapon-making material being put into circulation? Has the war increased Hussein's fame, and thus his ability to attract money, and with it, nuclear weaponry? What will the killing of many thousands of civilians during the war ultimately do to the political balance in the Middle East? Will the highly profitable business of rebuilding Kuwait encourage future wars to stimulate business? When questions are formulated with an awareness of systems, it is possible to ask whether beginning a supposedly containable war will ultimately lead to an uncontainable war.

Taking a systems notion into theory is significant in that it necessitates formulating constructs that work at the level of interconnectedness, with effects reverberating across and through links in a chain. The challenge is to model things like psychopathology, crime control, highways, or war in terms of their relationships. Separating war from its profitability is bound to disappoint. Or, as Rapoport said in a 1991 talk, after beginning to see the systemic pattern of war for profit by mapping out systemic interconnections, war can be redefined as "organized crime." As the cultural image of the soldier comes to be seen more as the gangster, perhaps the ideology of war will erode along with its funding.

The research directive is to look beyond: beyond the immediate, the first reaction, the simple, and toward the long term, the concerted playing of parts, the complex patterns of change in systems. This means, at its most basic, taking flowing continuous time dimensions into research designs. Measuring time one, time two, time three, and so on will not be as useful as looking at a process in continuous time. Analysts may punctuate data to pinpoint events, but this punctuation should never be confused with prejudging or inferring interconnectedness based on before-and-after measures. The key is to retain the sequence of systemic change patterns in one part through changes in all parts of the data. The move from phenomena to data should never reduce system characteristics. Wholeness and process must be retained.

In terms of everyday relevance, a systems notion allows thinking in sequence and with it resistance of simple short-term solutions to complex systemic problems. An apt example here is considering the long-term effects of medical intervention. A tragic illustration is Thalidomide, a drug that was given to pregnant women in order to reduce morning sickness but led to major birth defects in their children. The same principle is seen in addictions where, for instance, one substance is replaced with another. It is also illustrated by estrogen supplements like DES, which were prescribed to prevent miscarriage but were later shown to increase cancer risks in female offspring. Bringing the concept of interconnected reverberant change to personal choices in terms of health and lifestyle allows a means for questioning actions and in so doing avoiding ultimately destructive paths that appear on the surface as helpful.

UNIT

Unit refers to how we divide up the world in order to study it.

This issue considers where we make boundaries. What is included? What range is considered? Specifically for a wholes view, unit means making cuts or divisions such that relational wholes are retained. This means always keeping two or more parts and situations where relationships can be observed in total.

A wholes view means taking as the minimum unit two parts together. This issue is often neglected in the study of behavior where skin appears as a tantalizingly simple boundary to use to divide up phenomena. By far the most common approach to studying human behavior has been to collect data from individuals alone and then try to derive a collective picture of those individuals as a group by adding their individual scores. The principle of nonsummativity, which is the point of departure for a wholes view, renders the conventional approach to units a non sequitur. It does not follow.

If our point of departure is that the whole is greater than the sum of its parts, we cannot sum parts to find whole. Wholes, being our focus, must be hunted in a different fashion. It is perhaps here where so many attempts at systems approaches have gone astray. The principle of nonsummativity has been around since the time of Aristotle, but the practical means for applying it has yet to be developed. My sense is that this is tied to preoccupation with summative mathematics based in the principle of nomotheism, or universal properties. Historically the search for universals has been done via the observation of individual pieces. This dilemma has permeated the study of mathematics and physics at least since the time of Newton, leading to the classical issue of the "three body problem" (Lampton, 1992). The use of units as individual pieces, stars and planets in this case, is inevitably problematic because it does not capture the relational whole. Thus, moving to understanding a phenomenon of any more than two interrelated parts is confounding to summative-based mathematics. I think that this mode of inquiry may be related to notions of monotheism. One god, one law, OURS. Perhaps this idea of universality that predominates in the realm of conventional scholarship is rooted in one cultural view and is founded on the notion of a single universal frame of reference.

The avenue I propose for transcending the nomotheic is to focus on the immediate or particular rather than the universal or general. Instead of assuming the universal and working toward this hypothetical goal, shift to the particular and make its understanding the goal. To this end it is possible to propose the minimum rather than the ideal in terms of unit. Rather than infer an ideal universal and try to approximate this universal with successive degrees of error, instead work from known particulars. Take the example of gender, social constructions, and sex or biological characteristics. Gender is a co-emergent feature of groups of two or more parts, while sex is an individual attribute. Feminist scholarship has pointed out the inappropriateness of basing gender on sex. For example, denying women promotions because their sex makes them moody at certain times of the month would be inappropriate. This is a question of unit, trying to derive the characteristics of emergent wholes based on properties of individuals. This contradicts the basic point of departure of a wholes approach, nonsummativity. It is therefore inappropriate. So too is the attribution of the contextual to the individual. If sex does not equal gender then neither does gender equal sex. A wholes approach points to the possibilities in seeing a gender dynamic as a feature of relationships that is irreducible to the component members of those relationships.

The known particular becomes any two or more parts related such that change in one changes all. Division or unitization once this is the frame of reference for unit becomes tied to relevance in terms of the characteristic of interest, rather than the conventional focus on how well the unit represents the universal. So, for instance it is possible to define the unit of analysis as two spouses sharing a household when interested in emotional patterns that lead to abuse. This unit can be analyzed as a phenomena unto itself without concern for what the universal, average characteristics of spouse abuse are. Analysis grounded by a wholes approach may involve transporting constructs derived from the targeted unit to other units, but the major difference is that the relational unit is never broken down past the minimum of two interrelated parts.

In essence, particularity becomes as relevant a characteristic as similarity. The power of this distinction lies in remembering that a conventional nomotheic view of summation to average or universal rarely accounts for any more than 30 or 40% of variance in data so derived in the behavioral sciences. The belief that this minority explanation is relevant is just that, a belief. It is based on the assumption that the individual represents the universal. Therefore the common is judged based on the most frequent or average, even where this "common" trait explains a smaller fraction of the phenomena than it does not explain. The justification for this is that no single unexplained trait outnumbers the most common trait. This tradition has a long history.

There is a wholes alternative in terms of accepting the legitimacy of all units and explaining their particularity. The reference point for explanation becomes fit in context, an emergent whole as defined by the purposes of the analysis.

In intimate relations the relevance of this stance toward unit becomes apparent in the case of spousal abuse. The conventional approach has been to divide the relationship into a model of abuser and abused. Intervention follows this mindset by separating the individuals. Though this is an intuitively obvious means of proceeding, the pitfalls of this course of action become apparent in terms of unit. Even though spouses are divided, approximately half of spouse abuse involves former spouses. Further, there is high likelihood that spouse abuse will continue in subsequent relationships of individuals who have been in an abusive relationship. Attention to units of parts, to the neglect of wholes, misses the relational pattern. The importance of relational units becomes apparent when we see that this phenomena defies separation in that the pattern continues even after legal or physical separation. I am reminded of the story of the "antique" axe that has had two heads and four handles.

An interesting example of this in organizations is the story of Oskar Schindler's pot factory during WWII, as portrayed in the 1993 film *Schindler's List*. The factory was designed originally to make a profit from the Nazi war machine. It was so successful that Schindler was ready to abandon it once he had made a sizable profit. But Schindler's objectives changed, and the factory first designed to make money became a venture for losing money in order to resist the Nazi war regime and save the lives of the Jews working for Schindler.

One of the most important examples of the relevance of relational units has been in the analysis of international policy in nuclear armament. It is undesirable to separate the world into national units, many with their own nuclear arsenal. Instead one looks at the concept of nuclear armament as a relational phenomena whereby the fact that one country has nuclear weapons leads to others wanting and getting them. This leads to the idea that what is required is global disarmament. Because nuclear buildup rests not in the sum of countries, but rather in the relationships among them, only a relational solution will have a chance of working.

The importance of relational units in social policy shows up again in the story of the imposition of rent control legislation in Toronto. The intent was to increase the amount, quality, and affordability of rental accommodations in Toronto. Precisely the reverse has happened. Assuming that the units were two, renters and landlords, and neglecting the possibility that this was an interactive relationship, set the process roaring in the direct opposite of its intended direction. Because rents had to remain low, landlords began cutting back on repairs and improvements, sold, converted to condominiums, eliminated basement apartments, and so on. Little or no new rental accommodation was built because it was not financially feasible. Co-emergent with rising interest rates and recession, the house-building market slowed. Middle-class tenants could not afford to buy houses and so remained in "cheap" accommodations. Or, new middle-class tenants used their networks to secure new rent controlled housing, often paying "key money" (an illegal fee for securing rental accommodation). Middle-class people began investing in the burgeoning condominium market where they could afford to invest looking for a quick profit, but had no intention of living in the units. When the condominium market collapsed, co-emergent with the recent recession, these units went begging for rentals, but only in the high end market.

Failure to unitize the issue to the relational patterns that emerge between renters, landlords, and broader financial circumstances led to reduction of inexpensive, decent quality rental accommodations to the point that there is now a population the size of a city in itself, approximately 160,000 estimated in summer 1994 by the Daily Bread Food Bank in Toronto, which relies on food banks to survive. Both the proportion and amount of income needed for housing have increased drastically. The funds left over for food have therefore shrunk drastically, to the point where even people with jobs cannot feed themselves or their families, making them reliant on food banks. Units as relational wholes is derived from the principle of nonsummativity. If the whole is greater than the sum of its parts, the whole cannot be found by summing its parts. By extension this means retaining relational units in all phases of analysis. The units in the Gulf War were not the U.S. and Saddam Hussein, but rather their relationship. Analysis from this point is directed at explaining how the war emerged in a joint concert production. The unit of relevance may widen to consider various parts of the production, like the political changes in the Soviet Union, until a relevant pattern emerges.

The relevance of unit for theory is to underscore that it is a basic component of the theoretical approach that has direct implications for methods used to apply that approach. The question of unit is perhaps the most important linkage between a wholes approach to theory and a wholes approach to method. Because the question of unit as a relational whole is so intimately tied to nonsummativity, which is the point of departure for the wholes approach, breaking this link of legitimacy brings down the entire effort. As we move back and forth through theory, data, and analysis, relationships must be retained, or else the grounds for the approach disintegrate.

In practical terms for research, this means, at a minimum, gathering relational data, like observing spouses together, watching for joint patterns in organizational decisions, or looking at war as a zero sum game where all play. Statistical techniques for analyzing this form of data are not commonly available and need to be developed. If, however, the data is not relational to begin with there is no form of statistic that can salvage legitimacy. My directive is thus concentrated on the initial collection phase, with the hope that as more relational data sets emerge derivative analysis techniques will emerge as well.

Everyday examples of relevance crop up constantly, as in the case of a child training his or her parents. Take the example of a child learning the "f" word. He or she learns it for the first time, say from a playmate, comes home and says it to the parent. The parent immediately scolds the child who thinks, "AHA, this really is a useful word," and now knows how to control the parent's behavior. The behaviors of the scolding parent and swearing child must be seen as a unit in order to be understood. It also becomes apparent as I engage in my yearly concert production with nature as I try to achieve a weed-free lawn. If I use weed killer, I can't seed for a month, so on bare spots the weeds have time to take root. But, if I don't use weed killer, weeds take root in the healthy areas. The weeds and I have a relational unit that appears in patterns of weed proliferation. It is clear that they are winning at the moment.

Chapter 3

Causality

Causality refers to the inference of relationships between things
such that the combination brings about a result.

Pavlov created a revolution in the interpretation of human behavior through his experiments on dogs. He rang a bell and then fed the dogs. At first the dogs would salivate when they saw the food. After several repetitions the dogs began to salivate when they heard the bell. Pavlov concluded that learning was thus conditioned, the bell being the learned stimulus cue for the physical reaction of salivation. This was the beginning of classical conditioning being considered the basis of human learning, a belief that views learning as a black box, or input–output model, of human behavior. You introduce a stimulus (the bell), observe the reaction (salivation), and conclude that the bell caused the salivation. This illustrates the principle of linear causality in that a direct cause and effect relationship between stimulus and response is inferred.

Since the time of Pavlov, other experiments have been conducted. One researcher repeated Pavlov's experiment with one modification, elimination of the bell. The same results were observed. This researcher concluded that the bell was a stimulus for Pavlov, rather than the dogs. (Keeney, 1983)

The behaviorist school of thought, essentially grounded in a model of classical conditioning, took root with projects that explored variations on the theme. More complex tasks were designed in order to approximate the more complex tasks of human endeavor. Hence the rat maze came into wide use. Mice or rats were trained to find a food source in mazes constructed of varying complexity. The increases in speed with which a mouse would find the food in successive repetitions of the same task guided models of human learning.

During these times a creative graduate student decided to try a variation on the experiment to see if there was some variation with species. The issue involved discovering if there were cultural factors, properties of the joint experience of animals, that would alter learning patterns. Looking at the maze and thinking about cultural adaptation, the student decided to repeat the rat maze experiments with ferrets, creatures who had a cultural learning background suited to the business of going through narrow complex structures with twists and turns in order to find food for survival. When he did this the ferret found the food more quickly than any other animal had before. The student was elated and decided to run the experiment again immediately. However, the ferret ran quickly to the key juncture for finding the food, then went in the opposite direction, perhaps concluding that the food in this direction had already been caught. The student's supervisor pronounced the experiment a disaster. It was therefore abandoned.

Douglas Adams provides an interesting comment on the subject of causality in his writings about a time in the future when an Earthling is discussing the history of the Earth with a space traveler. The space traveler suggests that in fact mice have been experimenting on humans by complying with experiments in order to mislead the human race about its nature.

> How better to disguise their real natures, and how better to guide your thinking. Suddenly running down a maze the wrong way, eating the wrong bit of cheese, unexpectedly dropping dead of myxomatosis—if it's finely calculated the cumulative effect is enormous. (Adams, 1979/1992, p. 118)

Above, in circuitous fashion, I have tried to give a sense of the issues that are involved in a discussion of causality. What causes what? How do we figure it out? What are we assuming when we attribute cause? What is the relationship between posited causes and effects? These are the essential issues we treat when we address ourselves to causality. Below I will present the essence of one kind of wholes approach, namely a model of cybernetic, as opposed to linear, causality.

The stories above set up this presentation in that I began with the conventional approach to causality, namely that there is a direct linear relationship between cause and effect. Pavlov assumed that the stimulus he introduced, the bell, caused the effect, salivation, because the effect came after the cause. The essence of this is a model of "after-therefore-because."

The subsequent stories question the assumptions that underlay the conclusion that before and after are directly related: before causes after. First, in the case of the dogs who salivated without the bell, is the observed effect a result of the assumed stimulus or some other feature of the context? Second, with the ferret, can we assume that the relationship between cause and effect is linear and direct? Or, is there some characteristic of the phenomena being acted upon that mediates the outcome? Finally with the star traveler, we ask whether or not we can extrapolate from animal to human behavior, based on the assumption that there is no essentially differentiating characteristic that mediates in the process of cause and effect.

In an intimate relationship between parent and child, as the process of trying to get the child to sleep through the night begins, questions of cause arise. The child cries to get the parent's attention. If the parent responds, while the crying will be stopped in the short run, the sleeping through the night process will be delayed in the long run. Parents may give in to the short-term demand for attention and pick up the child in order to get some sleep, and then begin a new series of tactics like a large meal just before bed, keeping the child awake late to encourage sleeping to a reasonable hour, and so on. The question here is who is training who? What is the cause and what is the effect in a process that ultimately leads to a situation at the child's first birthday where no one is getting a full night's sleep?

In an organization such as a food store, suppose there is an attempt to increase the market share in jams and jellies. The store begins by slashing jam prices, even below cost. Shoppers flock to the store to buy jam. Increased demand means that prices can safely be raised, and higher priced exclusive products are introduced, while eliminating the low profit margin cheaper brands. Shoppers then reduce their purchases of jam, and maybe switch to homemade. Another store watches this process and slashes their cheap jam prices, drawing customers away from the original store. What is the cause and effect here? Can a simple A (lower prices) causes B (more profits) model be applied when a store is operating in a broader context of other interrelated parts? Perhaps observation of this complex contextual process in marketing is at the heart of moves to monopolize all food chains such that the process can be controlled since it would only have one part.

In the 1960s the U.S. and Canadian educational systems experienced unprecedented demand as the children of the post-war baby boom entered the system. The system was expanded rapidly by opening new schools and universities and hiring huge numbers of teachers. As education levels rose, birth rates dropped. Thus the system, so rapidly expanded in the 1960s, was downsized. School facilities were turned to other uses, university funding winnowed, and professors who left or retired were not replaced. However, as the 1980s rolled on, it became clear that women were not limiting their fertility so much as they were delaying it. A new "baby boomlet," appeared as persons who went through the education system in the 1960s began having children. So now in the 1990s we face a situation where there is extreme and increasing demand on the educational system and insufficient resources to serve this demand. What caused this?

The central relevance of issues of causality lies in causality's close link to intervention. Before a situation can be changed cause needs to be identified. Thus, the way in which these causes are defined will frame the way in which they are altered. If we decide the cause of problems in a relationship is one person's obesity, then fixing the problems means eliminating the obesity. If however, we see obesity not as the problem, but rather as an emergent surface projection of fundamental emotional pain in the relationship as a whole, then the focus of change becomes the emotional bond.

For theory, this means that any formulation that has a possible implication for intervention needs to be modeled in recognition of the overriding frame a particular epistemological stance toward causality presents. In research the question arises in terms of whether, and if so which, statistical representations are appropriate to the notion of causality. By and large, statistical models like linear regression (even if curved lines), log linear, or structural equation models assume a finite linear model of causality. This is implicit in the definition of dependent (held constant) and independent (allowed to vary) variables. One kind of variable is assumed to be caused and the other kind is assumed to be the cause. However, it is important to note that all of these procedures detect only correlation, and have no means of deciding on direction of relationships. The way the arrows point is purely a decision made by the analyst, and is not part of the statistic itself. The practical significance lies in thinking through whether one's actions have only direct linear effects or work in circular and circuitous fashion in the creation of co-emergent events. Does punishing a child increase or decrease the behavior, as he or she learns how to get attention? If women have to work twice as hard as men to get less rewards, under more difficult circumstances than men, could this lead to the feminization of poverty? Could planting the idea in public consciousness that war is "organized crime" lead to the dismantling of the U.S. war machine?

CYBERNETICS

Cybernetics is the study of the self regulating properties of systems.

The term *cybernetics* is derived from the Greek word "cyber," which reflects a notion of steering, or of one who handles an oar. It was picked by Wiener (1948) to name the observed ability of systems to steer themselves. Cybernetics becomes the refinement of theories to study processes by which systems self-regulate.

Targeting cybernetics, or patterns of self-regulation, is a significant step to studying the processes within a system that mediate in the stimulus-response linkage. This is why I include this idea in a chapter on causality. To begin to look at how systems of two or more interrelated parts steer themselves is to move away from a model of systems as passive entities, and toward seeing the way phenomena—be it organisms, species, machines, or climates—push back or create in ways that are not explained by knowledge of input and output alone.

Taking the example of human beings, this means moving away from a notion that a human is merely a point for relaying stimuli into responses. The human as relay model has been referred to as a "black box" view, comparing people to old camera boxes that merely redirect light without having any inherent means of modifying or creating. Symbolic interactionists and phenomenologists began challenging this notion of human nature. W. I. Thomas stated that "If men [sic] define situations as real, they are real in their consequences" (Wallace & Wolf, 1928, p. 240). This school of thought pointed out that because humans have the capacity for shared meanings or symbols, they are able to mediate outcomes based on emergent group properties. Thus phenomena such as runs on banks, or the aftermath of Orson Wells' *War of the Worlds* broadcast, where people believed the Earth had been invaded by aliens from outer space, could be explained. When it is acknowledged that things do not actually have to happen for reactions to occur, we can see why these collective actions take place. Furthermore, in the case of bank runs or recent stock market crashes and recessions, the belief that something will happen can make it happen. If it is perceived that a bank is about to fold, people run to get their savings to the point that the bank actually runs out of money. When people become fearful and cash out of the stock market, it crashes. Delay of major purchases out of trepidation for job security fuels recessionary curtailment of consumer spending.

Though the interactionists and phenomenologists may not have used the term cybernetics, their model of a human with reflexive self is wholly consistent with a notion of self-steering. In human systems, the ability to reflect upon one's self-worth in a view of merit tied to group definition, gives a form particular to human systems to the abstract notion of cybernetics. The legitimacy for use of a systems approach with the assumptions of symbolic interactionism lies in the conception of symbols as emergent properties of wholes not attributable to individuals alone. To take the example of self-reflection above, an individual may stand in front of a mirror evaluating himself or herself, but the content of those evaluations is not the individual's exclusive creation. Though he or she may choose a jacket from the closet, the decision of whether it is too masculine or feminine, casual or dressy, bold or conservative, will be mediated by an internalized notion of groups.

"Am I fat?" Asking this question, and the internal conversation a person has in the process of answering it, may lead to a whole series of cybernetic behaviors. Suppose this is asked soon after a romantic relationship has broken up. Feeling low self-worth, owing to feelings of failure, may lead to an answer of "Yes, I am fat," even if the person's weight has not changed. So they begin a diet, lose weight, but still feel fat. Feelings of low self-worth may remain and erode the resolve to lose weight, thus interacting with the physical body's adjustment to decreased food intake and leading to a gain in weight, often to levels above the original weight that began the pattern.

After coming under pressure from the observation that university "A" has the lowest proportion of women faculty members in the country, the vice president of the university decides to put an affirmative action hiring policy into place. Funding sources reward this initiative and give special money to allow the university to hire women. A central committee is set up to decide which of the 200 people who apply for the 20 available jobs are selected. Now 20 newly hired, primarily junior, women faculty begin full-time work. However, the patterns in the system that were co-emergent with a low proportion of women remain. The women are told they got their jobs "because they are women," are harassed by colleagues and students, are asked do service above levels asked of men, and their publication records are valued below men's. As time goes on, the women resign and go to other institutions, and are replaced by men in the positions funded to be held by women. Furthermore, these women tend to go to universities that had higher proportions of women faculty at the beginning of the process. University "A" remains with the lowest proportion of women faculty while the proportions increase steadily at other universities.

The Goods and Services Tax (GST), a regressive tax on virtually every retail and service transaction in Canada, was described by the federal government as a means of paying off the deficit. This tax on all transactions except stocks, banking, and other related business, meant that the relative cost to individuals was inversely related to the financial status of the person paying the tax. The less the income, the greater the proportion paid. Since the introduction of the GST the proportion of people living below the poverty level in Canada, those relying on welfare and food banks, has increased. The GST, introduced into a system prone to discrimination and limited, even inverse, financial mobility, may have contributed in co-emergent fashion to the increase of the deficit in that the money paid out for social services has increased while the taxable income has decreased because consumer spending is down.

How will the 1994 outbreak in India of bubonic plague, known colloquially as "the black death" of the Middle Ages in Europe, ultimately effect refugee and immigration policies worldwide? It is possible that pro-immigration and refugee policies will be targeted as exposing countries accepting immigrants and refugees from India to the danger of plague. In a country with systemic racism, this may fuel a political process that seeks to limit or eliminate immigration and refugee acceptance. Soon after the outbreak, pictures of immigration officials wearing medical masks appeared in newspapers.

In each instance the point is the same: there are patterns in systems of two or more parts that lead to self-regulation. This means that any action taken upon a system will reverberate through the existing patterns, and ultimate events will depend on those patterns rather than the stimulus. The notion of cybernetics in itself bears no preconception in terms of the direction steering will take. It is fundamentally the idea that these self-steering processes occur in systems and are the central problematic for theory refinement.

Cybernetic thinking is derived from an array of sources. Though I list Wiener at the central point in the formalized line of thinking on general systems theory, the idea has been around for centuries. There is the ancient Greek, roughly translated, "Never step in the same river twice, for as it remains the same it is constantly changing." Vaccination relies on a cybernetic notion by looking at the body's ability to steer toward lack of infection; thus, minor infection is used to initiate this process. Problems have cropped up with vaccination when the degree of steering ability has not been considered, leading to high incidence of side effects in undernourished populations. The adage, "You can take the person out of the country, but you can't take the country out of the person," reflects a notion of self-steering on a popular culture level. The term *cybernetics* becomes a means of giving form to all these observations in various sectors that may be known experientially and intuitively.

The theoretical task becomes finding concepts that are useful in explaining events of interest in the process of self-regulation in systems. In this vein, I will elaborate concepts such as positive and negative feedback, equifinality and multifinality, and agency. Taking cybernetics as the basis suggests formulating theories that begin to model patterns of cybernetic nature that can differentiate specific events. This allows a means of transcending sociology's micro–macro debate (Hanson, 1994b). Why *this* event with *this* input? Adding characteristics specific to the kind of system, human for instance, means refining ideas like parallogic (Hanson, 1989b) and emotion (Hanson, 1991b).

Research in this vein means, in the first instance, process. Time dimensions are crucial for any investigation of cybernetic process. In my own investigations of families with aged members, some of whom are identified as dementia patients, I found it possible to satisfy this time dimension by observing family members interacting together in continuous videotape samples of 10- to 15-minute segments to an approximate total of an hour for each family (Hanson,

1994e). The relatively short observation time frame satisfied me in terms of my quest for validity for two reasons. First, the cybernetic patterns I was looking for were so intense and pervasive that they manifested and repeated many times over in the 10-minute segments. Second, because the data were continuous, rather than slices taken at time intervals, the patterns were more easily spotted. Here the theoretical definition of the targeted phenomena determines how much and how long. Thus, for my current focus on the social construction of cancer and obstetric intervention, I am going back to 1900 for cancer and the 1950s for obstetrics, owing to the fact that I sense the patterns are slower to re-peat, and the fact that it is not possible to observe continuous pattern repe-titions given the massive data bulk that would be involved. The important direc-tion from cybernetics in this instance is to look for self-steering patterns in process in a mode appropriate to how the analyst theorizes the phenomena of interest.

Direct practical relevance of cybernetic thinking is found in observations about actions and inactions in systems of interrelated parts, and in how and where these systems steer. Has affirmative action brought gender equality closer or pushed it farther away? In what time frame? In what areas? Did George Bush's war on drugs decrease or increase drug use? Is the model here polio vaccine, which rendered the disease under control, or Prohibition, which led to black markets, crime syndicates, and widespread alcohol consumption across the population? By saying nothing when your spouse gets a new hairstyle, are you contributing to his or her low self-esteem?

ACTION AND INACTION

Action and inaction are equally causal in a system.

Because everything is related to everything in a system, there is no such thing as an action or inaction without causal status. Extending the notion of feedback, or linked interactive causal processes, means seeing that because it is process among parts, either doing something or doing nothing can fuel a sequence of either positive or negative feedback. Thus, there is no such thing as a behavior without causal significance in a system. In this sense action and inaction are of equal causal status.

If one does no weeding, the garden will fill up with weeds. If one cuts rather than pulls out weeds, or pulls weeds leaving the roots, the garden will fill with weeds. Here action and inaction can be seen as causal in the weed proliferation cycle.

Richard Needham once wrote about a character who described hell as a place where you gained one pound a day if you were dieting and two pounds a day if you were not dieting (Needham, 1968, p. 4). This captures quite succinctly the rebounding nature of dieting relative to weight gain. If people embark on a diet, it is likely that they will lose weight and then gain it all back and more. Thus, not trying to lose weight becomes a better long-term strategy for losing weight than trying to lose weight.

When a child comes home with a report card that is significantly improved over the previous ones and a parent says nothing, this ostensible inaction will have causal significance. The child who has been told constantly to improve grades, and after doing so gains no praise, may revert to earlier patterns. Or, if there is an emotional state of conditional love, whereby there is an unwritten rule that one must earn love based on conditions for approval that can, in fact, never be met, the child might try harder to get better grades to gain love, but wallow in low self-esteem and become obese.

Other variations on the idea that action and inaction are equally causal are illustrated in the realm of sexual relations. Here an inaction, like not using birth control or not using a condom, is causal in the sense that it feeds a causal feedback process that could lead to pregnancy or becoming infected with the HIV virus.

In the initial development of the microcomputer industry, IBM was noticeably absent. Many companies, including Apple, Hyperion, Osbourne, and Kaypro, emerged and went into competition for several years. Each company had its own unique operating system such that buyers were limited to only the software made by the company that also made their computer. Then IBM entered the market with its own operating system, DOS, licensed from Microsoft, which was also licensed to other software developers. By effectively standardizing rather than specializing, IBM was able to take over a large portion of the market and many of the original microcomputer companies folded, their machinery obsolete because it could not run DOS software. Historically, the only major exception among the original group of companies was Apple, which is now moving toward DOS operation in addition to their own unique system.

Here, IBM's initial inaction in the market had the long-term effect of establishing its ultimate market share and encouraging Apple to make its machinery capable of running DOS software. By waiting and watching at first, it was possible to make a long-term plan that was more ultimately successful than the short-term plans of smaller competitors. Some years from now history may record a different view of whether this was a good idea, as the population becomes more computer literate generally. It may be that reliance on large, established companies will be less attractive to consumers who paid more for IBM initially out of fear and the idea that buying a computer was a long-term commitment, like buying a refrigerator. Perhaps trends of constant upgrading and size reduction will lead to a computer market for obsolescence that more closely resembles that of automobiles rather than the lonely Maytag repairman.

Inaction in social policy and its causal significance can be spotted in terms of the spread of pollution in the Great Lakes. Lack of, or ineffective, regulation during the history of the cities that empty waste into the Great Lakes has meant that toxic substances can be dumped into the lakes or their feeding rivers and streams. The situation has gotten so bad that some beaches on the Great Lakes are closed for portions of the summer because the potential for infection is too high.

The notion that action and inaction are equally causal is derived from the basic definition of a system—two or more parts interrelated such that changing one part changes all parts. What this means is that any change reverberates through the system. Because parts are so inextricably linked, the possibility for causal significance from inaction arises. If one part does nothing, another may take up the part. Thus, lack of action leads to change.

As far as I know, this is my own argument. This idea contradicts the concept of "noise" used in engineering to refer to irrelevant data or parts occuring between input and output (Miller, 1968). To my mind the systems notion that everything is related to everything precludes noise if it falls within the theoretically defined unit of the system. There is no such thing as irrelevance in interrelated parts. My argument may reflect my focus on human groups rather than machines. Engineers may have clear goals for their machines and distortions or "noise" may be counterproductive to these goals. However, in human systems being goal-oriented may be a more contentious assumption. What should a human group be doing, or not? Noise, as a question of relevance, is an analytic decision. For me, it is less comfortable philosophically to decide what is relevant or irrelevant with human groups than with machines. In this sense I would argue that the concept of noise is not apt for the study of human groups.

A notion of action as causal is perhaps more intuitively obvious than inaction as causal. I began thinking about this possibility when stimulated by one of Watzlawick, Bavelas, and Jackson's axioms of communication, "the impossibility of not communicating" (1967, p. 72), or the extension, you ". . . cannot not communicate" (p. 75). These authors elaborate this notion in terms of the concept of nonverbal metacommunication, and point out that there is no such thing as not communicating, because even lack of talk is communication, as is the body language that accompanies this nontalk.

I extend this axiom into a general principle that action and inaction are equally causal. This is a derivation of the definition of system, an extension of a systems model of human communication. This principle has an impact on theory by suggesting the challenging task of modeling ostensible nonentities in the form of inactions. The dilemma is how to model something that *is not* rather than *is*. The directive is to model inaction in causal feedback loops. Look constantly to where the holes in wholes lead, the patterns and events they spawn through the other parts of a system. Because of the principle of interrelatedness it is possible to trace nonthings. This is demonstrated by various forms of medical testing. The discovery of things that are not happening and are leading to problems that show up in other things is a common occurrence. The pancreas is "inacting" insulin leading to elevated blood sugar levels, while the arteries are inacting the free flow of blood, which leads to shortness of breath, and the liver inacting the filtration of blood leads to elevated blood toxins. Diagnosis means looking at symptoms like high blood sugar, panting, or blood toxins, and inferring an inaction.

Perhaps the metaphor of medical testing can be applied to research methods. The challenge is to move into models of causality that can somehow capture inaction. One possibility is to unitize data for statistical analysis such that relational wholes are treated as the unit. Sequences extend as far as possible along a continuum of action, reaction, inaction, counteraction, counterinaction, and so on. This may mean moving to data sources that can capture directly interactive feedback processes, like angiograms, which allow watching the actual process of blood flow through the heart and arteries in entirety, rather than inferring the process based on input and output levels, heart sounds, or blood enzymes. In the behavioral sciences this has been approximated by use of videotaped interaction samples of persons acting in concert (Hanson, 1994e). In my work I have moved from analysis of these wholes to transportable constructs. I am just now exploring possibilities for statistical analysis of data so derived. Initial explorations have involved using data listed for individuals, in this case coders, cumulatively by looking at the patterns and correlations rather than the correlations themselves (Hanson, in press-a, in press-b).

"Damned if you do, damned if you don't." This familiar saying sums up succinctly the principle that the causal status of action and inaction are of equal significance. Seeing any individual action, one's own or that of others, as inextricably linked to a causal web provides a means of evaluating choices in one's actions and inactions. When we see that doing nothing may have just as much effect as doing something, attitudes toward inaction may change. For instance, suppose you think a university professor is doing an excellent job with the courses you are taking, but others in the class hate his or her approach. If you do not write a letter of praise, while the others write letters of criticism, then you may be contributing through inaction to the professor refusing to teach the course, or being denied tenure. This principle encourages people to think about their inactions and the ultimate events that they may spawn.

CO-EMERGENCE

*There are certain things that exist as a joint production
and can therefore be seen as co-emergent.*

What is the sound of one hand clapping? Is there such a thing as "defense" without two or more parts working together to sustain the phenomenon? Co-emergence refers to phenomena of interest that are a cooperative, or joint, creation.

One of the simpler illustrations of this concept is a seesaw, or teeter-totter. The creation of play on the device needs two people acting together. If one person decides to be mean and jump off, the other will be dropped to the ground and the game cannot go on. So it is with the prisoner's dilemma, the zero sum game, and its relevance to game theory in peace and conflict studies. The essence of the prisoner's dilemma is a situation where two people are suspects of a crime they did together. The suspects are put in separate cells in jail, approached individually for questioning, and are not allowed to talk to one another. The police go to each suspect individually and say that "If you act as a witness, tell that your partner did it, we will let you go free and your partner will get a 20-year jail term. However, if you don't help us we will convict you both and you will both get 5 to 10 years." The prisoner's dilemma becomes whether to "rat" on the partner for personal gain or stay quiet. The best solution for both is if they both stay quiet. However, this only works if both stay quiet. If one chooses silence while the other tells all, the one being quiet gets 20 years and the other goes free. Thus, the prisoner's dilemma is a co-emergent phenomena that arises from a situation where the actions of individuals must be seen in terms of how these individual strategies fit events in the phenomena as a whole.

This analogy becomes very important in the consideration of peace and conflict studies because a nuclear war with two protagonists bears the same characteristics as the prisoner's dilemma. Massive effort has gone into trying to calculate the best strategy for "defense." Is it better to strike first with minimum domestic casualties and annihilate the enemy? Or, do you do nothing and wait for them to strike you? Recalling my discussion in this book's introduction, the movie *War Games* demonstrates this with its story about a massive computer that controls the launch of nuclear weapons and constantly calculates the "best" outcomes for war. An unwitting intervention by a teenage computer whiz, who thinks he has tapped into a new video game, starts the computer on the war sequence for real. At the last moment a nuclear launch is avoided when the general chooses not to "push the button," while the Soviets independently reach the same decision. It ends with the conclusion from the computer, "Interesting game. The only way to win is to not play."

A parallel illustration of the principle of co-emergence can be found in the pattern of spousal violence. There is a cyclic pattern whereby tensions build until some incident sparks violence. Over time spouses learn to read the cycles, and some report that they can see it coming, so they provoke the violence to get it over with, sometimes in order to make sure they do not have visible injuries at the time of some special occasion. This pattern co-emerges between spouses as a characteristic of their relationship. The importance of co-emergence in understanding this phenomenon is seen when spouses are separated in order to try to stop the violence. The pattern often co-emerges despite this with large proportions of "spousal" violence between ex-spouses.

Steven Jobs sold his Volkswagen van in order to get the money to build a prototype of a microcomputer. Apple computers co-emerged as a contender in the computer marketplace. This initial entrance by Apple brought the concept of microcomputers to the forefront. I remember seeing one of the original Apple models in 1981. It was about the size of a large desk. As the concept became popular all sorts of competitors came into the market. Apple revamped and Steven Jobs was eventually pushed out of the company he founded (Rose, 1989). As competition increased there was a move to make computers smaller. Thus any large model quickly disappeared from the market. In 1983 I bought a Kaypro II that is still sitting on my desk. It is about 3 feet wide by 1 foot deep, weighs 25 pounds, and has a Random Access Memory (RAM) of 64K. I am writing this book on my recently acquired Sanyo notebook, which is about the size of a large book, fits in my briefcase, and has 5 megabytes of RAM. It cost about the same as the Kaypro did in 1981, so it is less expensive in adjusted dollars and has approximately 80 times the capacity. My new equipment is a co-emergent phenomena in that introduction of a new idea, microcomputers, by Apple led to the relational dynamics of market competition and consumer responses in the form of replacing equipment with new versions that were smaller, cheaper, and had increased capacities. This can be understood in terms of co-emergence: the push-pull, action-counteraction dynamic of a competitive marketplace.

Co-emergence gives a form to the wholes point of departure, that the whole is greater than the sum of its parts. Such wholes are co-emergent in that they exist between, rather than within, individual parts of a system. A notion of co-emergence is thus derived from this basis of a systems approach. The key addition of this construct lies in providing a term to capture the idea that emergence is a joint production. As such it offers a systems-grounded alternative to a notion of emergence. By working "co" into the word directly, it provides a kind of emergence that is consistent with a systems approach.

Co-emergence becomes relevant to theory on two fronts. First, it gives further form and elaboration to a notion of causality that departs from the linear. A conventional linear model of $A + B + C = X$ does not allow for the possibility of co-emergence in that the component sums do not explain the co-emergent event. Second, it allows modeling of the nature of co-emergent events. Constructs in line with this are found in equifinality and multifinality, which capture two different kinds of co-emergent patterns.

Research directives directly follow these two theoretical implications. A model of co-emergence demands statistical procedures that can capture this nonsummative property of systems. My own thinking in this area has been spurred in the direction of trying to alter the ways in which statistics are used. Initially I have tried using data units that are co-emergent, such as joint patterns in intimate relationships. What remains to be worked out are statistics that work on nonsummative principles. The principle of co-emergence applied to research means retaining relational units at all phases of the process. Most fundamentally this means keeping parts together as wholes, from data collection right through analysis. Specifically it can be used to argue for continuous time observation in order to allow researchers to see how things co-emerge.

In practical terms this means looking at sequences of events over time repetitions until a pattern emerges. For example, take a time sequence on defense spending. What actions by the U.S. co-emerged with actions and inactions by the former Soviet Union and ultimately with Iraq, Iran, and Kuwait? Is there one guest who always provokes a member of the family to argue? What led to the soccer riots in Great Britain? Have you ever seen someone suffering from an event like a career failure, who rushes immediately into a romantic relationship that appears to feed low self-esteem and destructive behavior patterns? The directive in each instance is to see how specific events act in concert to produce some co-emergent phenomena. In practical terms it is possible to see how the principle of co-emergence operates in personal relationships. Why does someone fantasize in fond terms about a past relationship, which he or she broke off because it was destructive to their self-esteem, right after a recent relationship stalls? What sets off self-destructive behavior in a loved one? Why is it they become abusive toward people who show that they like them, right after some career setback? What unexpected side effects occur when you set a co-emergent process in motion, for example, by telling someone they should lose weight? In terms of everyday life this means being aware of how actions and inactions may feed into an interactive process that leads to unexpected, unintended, or even the obverse of intended, co-emergent events.

AGENCY AND THE IMPOSSIBILITY OF BLAME

Blame is incompatible with a general systems theory approach in that it violates the principle of nonsummativity.

One of the contributions of this book to the body of thinking on systems theory is the idea that blame is an inconsistent notion within a wholes approach because it necessitates a summative approach. Blame is therefore incompatible with a general systems theory approach. It is theoretically inconsistent and therefore an impossibility within wholes epistemology.

Blame involves two notions: being able to assign cause in the form of responsibility and being able to separate cause from effect. Both enterprises are incompatible within a wholes approach. The notion of blame involves separating parts of a system in order to isolate the causal factor and then attributing responsibility to that factor. This requires two aspects of epistemology, separating parts from a whole and finite linear causality. Neither are appropriate to a wholes approach.

I use agency as an issue of efficacy in the sense of the ability to act or exert power or control. This is inherent in a notion of blame because the attribution of blame would seem to require the assumption that someone or something is first able to act and second able to exert control or power, before a notion of responsibility for an action can be attached. The question of whether or not a part can act is not questioned by a wholes approach; whether or not a part can control or exert power is. Because properties of context exist only as emergent wholes any power attributed to a part is moot. Thus, the question of whether one part does or does not control and in what way is not a question at all. Rather, it is a non sequitur to the point of departure that the whole is greater than the sum of its parts.

In the question of agency and the impossibility of blame seems to lie a close alliance with tendencies to moralize or idealize, also inherently unnecessary to a systems approach. The importance of a theoretical stance without the inherent capacity for blame becomes apparent by returning to my discussion of the 1991 escalation of the war in the Persian Gulf in terms of a blame-attributing process. Who or what caused it: politicians, industrialists, the military, or the media? All throughout the buildup there was extensive effort on the part of the U.S. to plant and reinforce the idea that they were on the defensive. "Hussein started this. We are acting only to save others, not as the aggressors." Furthermore, it was constantly stressed that while the vast majority of force was coming from the U.S., they were acting as "coalition forces." The wholes alternative would be to say that the question of cause, and with it blame, is not relevant. The important aspect here is how the process emerged via a concert production between various parts like Hussein, the industrial military alliance, George Bush, the Soviet Union, public opinion polls, the United Nations, and so on. At the alleged "end" of the war there were many thousands of civilian casualties in addition to military casualties. The concept that war can still take place with conventional weaponry has been planted. There was an immense expenditure from all countries involved that diverted funds from other priorities. Hussein is still in power. The U.S. military returned to the Gulf in 1992.

What is the analytic point of trying to establish who or what is to blame for the war? The wholes alternative is to instead look at how any variety of stimuli can lead in an equifinal process to war when the patterns in the system as a whole are so prone to this result. The power of this kind of thinking lies in seeing that there is little to be gained in blaming isolated parts when the system shows a marked ability to replace parts. Witness the thawing of the Cold War. When the defense threat to the U.S. posed by the Soviet Union began to diminish, a new enemy arose, like clearing out one set of weeds while a new one springs up; this continues unless the system is altered, say (in the case of weeds) by putting down a plastic barrier or (in the case of international relations) holding to a global peace treaty that relies on economic sanctions. The answer to my question, "What is the point of trying to establish who or what caused the war?" can be seen from a systems approach as political, rather than analytical. The issue becomes instead what are the patterns that are involved in trying to attribute blame, rather than the issues of blame. Who benefits from blaming whom?

The importance of the systems shift to discarding blame as a target of analysis, making it an "un-question," comes up when we go through examples and watch each time for the ways in which the search for blame itself can inflame or exacerbate nonsummative, co-emergent processes in interrelated systems. In my own work on senile dementia in family contexts, I observed a pattern whereby family members seem to be in a desperate search for blame, in the sense of explanation for emotional distress (Hanson, 1991c). In this process, the "cause" is constructed to be the illness of one family member who becomes the patient. In the course of the social construction of the idea that *the problem* is this person's illness, even ostensibly sane and appropriate, and behavior is reinterpreted for the person into the illness category. This even extends to the judging of feelings or opinions as wrong or inappropriate, and therefore they are part of the problem. This sets up a situation where the person considered to be the patient has no means of being correct, not even of having correct feelings. The search for blame in the form of a person's illness thus increases and ingrains illness behavior.

I was told a story about an ideologically based health help center that was staffed with a number of people highly qualified in the dynamics of counseling and conflict resolution. Within the first year of opening, the center was in serious strife, with work not going on, people threatening to resign, high stress levels, and general dissatisfaction. The consensus among the staff was that the director was the problem. A high-level administrator intervened and decided to hire an external conflict resolution expert and send the entire staff on a retreat to try to work out these problems. The only conclusion of the retreat was to fire the conflict resolver and ask that the director be fired as well. Eventually the director was forced to resign and blacklisted from working in the immediate locale. A new director was hired and within a short time the center was in the grips of the very same problems that spawned the retreat and led to the departure of the first director. The second director had a nervous breakdown. In sum, the process of search for blame in a single part, based on the assumption of agency, may in fact have exacerbated elements of the system in this center as a whole. This led to a negative feedback process whereby incredibly high levels of stress and conflict were maintained in the long run. Attention was focused on the search for a cause to the neglect of the interactive system patterns that worked toward distress.

Though it will be some time before the full pattern of effects is known, allow me to recap and predict how the pattern of blame-attributing for declining retail sales in the province of Ontario, Canada, might lead to the spiraling decline of retail sales in Ontario. The combination of the Free Trade Agreement with the U.S., the North American Free Trade Act, and the Canadian Goods and Services Tax appear to have spawned equifinal, varying stimuli leading to the same output, declining levels of consumer spending in Canada. In response, outcries for legalizing Sunday shopping intensified. Across-the-border shopping in Buffalo, New York, the closest U.S. market to the largest concentration of Canadian shoppers, increased on Sundays, co-emergent with the widespread publicity Sunday shopping and cross-border shopping had received.

Sunday shopping has since been legalized in Ontario, Canada. Stores are now able to open on Sunday. My prediction here is that in the overall pattern of decreasing markets for retail spending, stores will have to decrease profit margins or raise prices in order to recoup the extra costs of staying open an extra day each week (labor, maintenance, utilities). Competition will lead to the consolidation of smaller retail operations into larger operations in that the smaller the margin, the larger the sales volume needed to maintain profits. Given that the Canadian population is approximately 10% of the size of the U.S. population, it is therefore likely that U.S.-based companies will come out ahead and be able to keep prices lower than their Canadian counterparts. This is seen in the recent takeover of Woolworth and Woolco stores by Wal-Mart from the U.S. The relative price differences will continue to increase, because U.S. companies operating in Canada do so at greater cost than in the U.S. Also, the taxes added to retail spending in Ontario total 15%, which is comprised of a 7% provincial tax plus an 8% federal goods and services tax. This will encourage even more cross-border shopping. The search for a single cause for declining Canadian retail sales, lack of Sunday shopping, and its alteration, may in the future lead to acceleration of the decline in Canadian retail sales co-emergent with the increasing market shares for U.S.-based retail companies operating in Canada.

The message in each of these instances is that the search for blame can lead to events that are the obverse of those intended. Looking to find the cause of emotional pain can increase it. Trying to prevent someone or something from causing a war leads to a war. I argue that the search for blame, via agency, is not only inconsistent with a wholes approach, it may be unwise.

The message for theory is that it is important to think in terms of the process of theory building as part of its social historical context. It may be useful to consider the ideologies and emotions of those who create theories. This is echoed in Rapoport's call for the redemption of science through recognition of social and moral responsibility of scientists (1989) and in Wiener's book *Cybernetics* (1948). In research it is possible to return to the fundamental epistemological underpinnings of inquiry and ask whether the search for linear cause and effect relationships with the intent of assigning cause and with it, blame, is a process that contains the seeds for possible amplification of systems processes. A systems approach provides an alternative means of conceptualizing the goals of research as well the process of achieving such goals. Look for pattern as opposed to cause, process rather than product, events rather than outcomes. In terms of the everyday, it is possible to think about where the need to assign blame derives. Could it be an overlay of fundamental religiously-oriented causal modes about cause and effect regarding concepts like good and bad, salvation and damnation? Where does the general search to moralize in terms of right and wrong and, in so doing, assign blame via agency co-emerge?

Chapter 4

Change

Change is an issue of what is altered or not.

The more things change, the more things stay the same.
Plus ça change, plus c'est la même chose!

Change is a question of what changes and what stays the same. These popular sayings capture in slightly different ways the concept of change from a wholes approach. A wholes approach to change involves seeing that change is a question of difference and similarity, dynamic and static, alteration and continuity. The key is to see the issue of change as having both component issues, what changes and what stays the same, rather than just change alone.

This is a more flexible and dynamic approach than a conventional view of linear, evolutionary change in the sense that it does not necessitate a progress or advancement ideology. Neither does it assume that change or nonchange is inherently good or bad. Instead it focuses on theorizing patterns of change and nonchange. With a wholes approach different sorts of questions arise. Has the development of nuclear weapons been change or stability and in what sense? Have they promoted or prevented war? Has the spread of medically-mediated pregnancy and birth management techniques such as amniocentesis and cesarean sections changed the safety of the process? If so, has giving birth become safer or more dangerous in the sense that intervention itself presents dangers?

A systems concept of change allows moving to models of overall patterns of change rather than assuming any observed difference is change. It stresses the importance of time and process in determining what the relative patterns of alteration and continuity mean in the long run. Rather than look at the immediate reactions to the two most recent stock market crashes, look instead to whether or not these specific events are part of a long-term process that is maintaining the relative gap between the wealthy and the poor and restricting upward mobility. The focus becomes whether or not short-term changes are in fact contributing to long-term stability of a pattern of increasing social discrimination. A wholes approach provides the flexibility to see even a pattern of change, in the sense of increase or decrease, as nonchange.

This stance allows spotting the cyclic and generational patterns that are observed in pathologies tied to intimate relationships. While a great deal of alteration and shift can be observed in the short term, in the long run the pattern is the same. It is a clinical truism that I have yet to see fully researched that there is generally only one patient in a family at a time, but both the person who is the patient and the condition may change over time. Thus you might see a pattern whereby there is an alcoholic parent who stops drinking, but enters into an incestuous relationship with a child. This child leaves for college or work and another child becomes anorexic. The child who departed enters into a relationship with an alcoholic. Drinking behavior goes down but premenstrual tension co-emerges. There have been a number of changes, yet the pattern of distress behavior continues, even into new relationships.

A friend recounted the story of his Boy Scout troop. The leader of the troop was not liked by a sizable section of the troop. This group banded together and plotted the overthrow of the leader. With a careful strategy they managed to get him out. However, within a few months the leader was back as leader and his position was now more secure after having survived the "coup." Was there any change in the long run, even though there was change in the short run? In this instance it is possible to see how the short-term change against the leader ultimately led to the long-term change of increasing the strength of the leader and disbanding his opposition. In total, the process maintained and solidified the pattern of this leader's control.

Social policy and upward mobility is an interesting example of the principle of change—what changes and what stays the same. A true story: a man immigrates to North America from Europe in the 1920s and begins work as a barber. He changes his surname to a more anglicized version and marries a woman who has also emigrated from Europe. They buy a small four-room house in a working-class neighborhood. Their first-born son is the only one of his friends to attend college. He gets a bachelor's degree in engineering, marries, starts his own ultimately very successful business, and moves to a big, elaborate fifteen-room house in an upper middle-class neighborhood in the suburbs. His daughter goes to college, gets a Ph.D., and becomes a university professor. She notices that her grandparents' house in the now trendy upper middle-class area of the city is for sale and realizes that she cannot afford to buy it. What has changed and what has stayed the same?

The derivations of a wholes approach to change are as much intuitive and experiential as they are intellectual. Experience with time, both in terms of personal and population aging suggests the need for a flexible approach to change.

It is possible to argue that as more and more people live longer and longer, the increased view of time and process provides sensitivity to the process of ostensible change in the long-term pattern of continuity.

Parents watch the process of children striving to get ahead, only to be in a position of less financial security than themselves. Entrepreneurs watch the cyclic trends of the marketplace and wonder if all the massive gains in their businesses, only to be followed by stagnation or bankruptcy, have actually gained them any relative ground. People who work hard to achieve the resources to move out of crime-ridden inner city neighborhoods find that in general crime rates are increasing everywhere, fueled by the segregation of the poor and the middle class. The long-term accumulation of consumer goods has co-emerged with a massive global problem for disposing of outdated goods. Perhaps the ultimate example is war machinery that becomes obsolete almost immediately and is therefore "garbage."

My own current dilemma is my old Kaypro computer, which represented highly sophisticated technology of the early 1980s but by today's standards is likened to the stone tablet and chisel. It does everything I need it to do but has become effectively useless not because of itself, but rather because I can get new machines that do more faster, like the one on which I am typing this book. Even giving the old machine away is problematic in that I would handicap the user for current competition. This raises interesting systems grounded questions about how the concept of "garbage" relates to ongoing patterns of what changes and what stays the same. Is the acceleration of garbage pile height positively related to increases in military spending over time? Is garbage pile height in industrialized nations correlated over time with increases in famine and infant mortality in developing nations?

The relevance of this to theory is to build the dimension of time into models. At the most basic level this means looking for models of ongoing processes that can capture these long-term patterns of change and nonchange. Feedback, multifinality, and equifinality, discussed below, are constructs directed at this aspect of a wholes approach. The key is to work to develop constructs that provide language that works as a process rather than linearly or in finite sequence. To this end, in my work on mental illness I have elaborated the theoretical construct of "patienting" as an ongoing joint social construction process in intimate relationships, which leads to events like hospitalization or recovery (Hanson, 1991c). This is a major epistemological shift to seeing events rather than outcomes. Events become analytically defined punctuation points to which attention is directed, all the while recognizing that these are mere snapshots of an ongoing process. The tendency to look for the result, endpoint, or outcome is thus abandoned in favor of seeing patterns in processes.

Longitudinal research with continuous time frames is suggested by the notion of change. Seeing what changes and what stays the same means allowing a sufficient time frame to capture the back and forth sway. Furthermore, the temptation to unitize and in so doing prejudge the time frame for patterns must be resisted as much as possible. Practicalities like deadlines, funding ceilings, and getting tenure detract from the desire to make research frames into ongoing processes. However, in order to best approximate the phenomena they are designed to understand, resist. Recently some North American funding organizations such as the U.S. National Institute on Mental Health (NIMH) and the Canadian Social Sciences and Humanities Research Council (SSHRC) have begun to recognize this dilemma and have acted by extending their funding time unit from one year to three or more years. These types of strategies need to be encouraged using the principles of a wholes approach.

In personal terms the notion of change as continuity in the face of alteration provides a means of framing some of the dilemmas of personal growth. Escape from one bad relationship into another, which appears like a change but maintains a pattern of conditional love and with it downward-spiraling self-esteem, can be examined critically before making life choices. Similarly, the move to acquire property or possessions as a means of improving life or reducing distress in a relationship can be framed by looking back and projecting forward patterns in one's own life and in the lives of others.

FEEDBACK

Feedback refers to the ability of a system to reintroduce output as input.

Through the process of feedback, a system is able to make indications to itself and in so doing, steer itself. It captures the process whereby causality, rather than being finite and linear, is interactive and continuous. Norman W. Bell suggested to me that in this sense we can think of feedback, feeding back onto a system, as "feed forward" as well. There is an action, then a reaction, then a reaction to the reaction, then a reaction to the reaction to the reaction, and so on. In total the process of feedback steers the system.

This notion, de rigueur in alternative forms of health care, came into view in Western medicine in the form of "biofeedback". It had long been "known" in conventional Western medicine that certain of the body's systems were autonomic, or not consciously controlled by the person (blood pressure, the nervous system, heart rate). However, with the influx of alternative perspectives it became apparent that these systems could be controlled if a feedback system was set up such that a person could monitor his or her output of rates from these systems. It was shown that a person could lower heart rate and blood pressure by learning thought control and relaxation techniques. By showing the person a good or bad indicator of output, this was introduced as input to the system, prompting a new reaction; in total steering the system in the desired direction. This process is very similar to the gas consumption monitors that were put in cars during the gas shortages of the late 1970s and early 1980s. There were red (high consumption) and green (low consumption) lights put on the dashboard right in front of the driver. By monitoring behavior such as abrupt or gradual acceleration, speed, and gear shifting patterns, the driver could learn to drive in a fuel-efficient manner by watching the lights. In both instances the point is the same, an output is fed back to the system as input, allowing a system to steer itself.

Feedback comes into play in the course of a pattern of behavior among spouses. One spouse withdraws. The other nags and presses. The first withdraws further. The other nags harder and louder. The first retreats outside. Both enter into a "seesaw" pattern that can only go on when both play. It could also be seen in two companies vying for their share of the pizza market. One company offers a single order number for the whole region. The other reacts by offering "Two-for-One Tuesdays." The original counters with "Unlimited Toppings Wednesdays." Then it continues with "10% off Coupons" and "We Accept all Competitor Coupons." Then comes a new player, "McPizza." In total, the action, reaction, and counter reaction of the pizza competitors steers the system, perhaps to the point in this scenario where the profit margins become so low that only a mass international operation can survive in the market.

One of the more frightening recent examples of a feedback process has been in the communication of AIDS. In the early stages of discovery, it became apparent that most of the people who had the disease were gay men. This spawned the term GRIDS (Gay Related Immune Deficiency Syndrome) (Shilts, 1987). As time went on and research accumulated, it became apparent that anyone could catch the virus, regardless of sexual orientation. However, the initial output of associating the virus with male homosexuality fed back into the system. Events in this process have involved the continuation of high risk behavior for heterosexuals in the belief that they are not at risk for AIDS because they are not homosexual. A recent offshoot of this is that, at present, infection rates are growing among heterosexual women. Further, for those living with the virus, it evokes the prejudices and discrimination associated with promiscuity or homosexuality, which add to difficulties in coping with the virus. This is illustrated poignantly in the 1993 movie *Philadelphia*. Actor Tom Hanks portrays a lawyer who is HIV positive, conse-quently loses his job, and is forced to fight a legal battle while living with the AIDS virus.

The ability of systems to steer themselves provides a means of understanding the way in which biomedical intervention has led either to unanticipated side effects or ultimate worsening of the conditions it tried to alleviate. The wide-spread use of antibiotics is co-emergent with "superbugs," bacteria that are re-sistant to antibiotics (Priest, 1994). There are strains of syphilis that are now resistant to penicillin. Rats that are poison resistant exist. Many of the drugs used to treat cancer have since been attributed to causing it (Tomatis, 1990, p.149).

POSITIVE AND NEGATIVE FEEDBACK

*Positive feedback leads to change
while negative feedback leads to no change.*

Above, I have defined and illustrated in detail the general concept of feedback, reintroducing output as input in the process of steering. Now I shall develop two types of feedback, positive and negative, which lead to change or no change, respectively, to elaborate a conception of the directions in which the process of feedback goes.

Positive feedback refers to a feedback process where there is change. Nega-tive feedback refers to a feedback process where there is no change. The deter-mination of whether a process is positive or negative lies solely in whether there is change or not, regardless of the nature of the inputs and outputs. This is illustrated in Figure 1, which uses a triangle, the mathematical symbol for change and the popular format for yes and no.

Take the example of the process of athletic coaching. The goal here would generally be change in the direction of performance improvement. However,

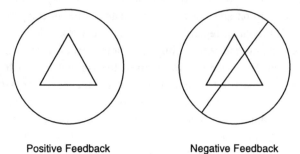

Positive Feedback   Negative Feedback

Figure 1 Positive and negative feedback.

and this is the important point, change is achieved by both reward and punishment. The coach watches a performance. In order to change the performance for the better, he or she both rewards, praises the good parts, and punishes, criticizes the bad parts with suggestions for improvement. As the coach works with different athletes, it becomes apparent that some respond better to constant criticism while others respond to constant praise and some to a combination of both. The important point is that the process is all positive feedback, regardless of whether reward or punishment makes up the individual inputs and outputs.

In general the continuity of a system is served by both negative and positive feedback. The human body itself displays this in terms of balance. In order to stay "still," the body adjusts itself back and forth in a continuous pattern of flex and readjustment. You can experience this by trying to draw a straight line first very quickly and then by going the same length while counting slowly to 20. The slowly drawn line will likely show the back and forth sway. You can then hold the paper with arm outstretched AND rigid and close your eyes. When you open your eyes, the paper will likely be vibrating. It was knowledge of this pattern of positive and negative feedback that led early photographers to use a rigid brace for the human head to keep it still during the several second long exposures required to fix an image. This is part of the reason for the stiff appearance of people in old photographs.

Never changing and always changing are potentially equally destructive. Here enters the possibility for analyzing problem situations. By focusing on the negative and positive feedback processes in a system, it is possible to trace the roots of problems. A family therapist may spot a pattern whereby a child, now in his or her twenties, has been kept dependent. Sexuality has been denied, independence has been restricted, and career growth has been curtailed such that this person is underachieving in school, is overweight, and has difficulty with intimacy. The changes associated with growing up, learning new things, and making friends have been counteracted with a negative feedback process directed toward a constant state of childhood.

A heating repairperson arrives in the dead of winter to find the occupants of a house dressed in shorts and t-shirts. A thermostat, which is designed to be a combination of positive and negative feedback—heat on, heat off, maintaining an overall pattern of a temperature range around a set midpoint—has embarked on an unfettered positive feedback process. Some crossed wire meant that the output of temperature kept giving the signal for more heat. Thus, the temperature kept rising. This would also be a positive feedback process if it were summer and the household members were dressed in their mitts and parkas due to an out-of-control air conditioner.

It is perhaps within the notion of positive and negative feedback where a

wholes approach takes its most obvious departure from conventional mechanistic and moral epistemologies. Freeing analysis from a simplistic view of reward and punishment allows seeing a more dynamic long-term process, rather
than a simple finite cause and effect sequence. Furthermore, it allows going
beyond the view that punishment stops things from happening and reward encourages it. The importance of this shift in thinking becomes apparent in the
area of criminality, where punishment tends to maintain or increase criminal
behavior. This is the central tenet of labeling theory. Labeling someone a criminal sets off a process of self-definition as a criminal, ingraining this pattern and
encouraging a career of crime.

The systems shift of epistemology regarding causality provides a means of
suspending moral, cultural, or ideological judgment about what is right and
wrong. By focusing on feedback processes as negative or positive, leading to no
change or change, there is a way of seeing the complexities in this process in
terms of how they work in the system, rather than in terms of external judgments. To be overly concerned with the wrongness of incest, for example, re-
stricts the analyst's ability to see what incest behavior may mean to a family,
what emotional distress has led to it. To merely judge without seeing as the
participants do is to limit the ability to understand. Feedback can be traced to
the intuitive observation *Plus ça change, plus c'est la même chose*: the more
things change, the more they stay the same. More formal connections are found
in the development of an ecological view of biological systems. Careful attention is directed at how input and output feed back, and feed forward. It is
possible to view swings in cycles of population size in species as positive and
negative feedback in order to understand the long-term picture and in so doing
avoid destructive intervention. Suppose the massive surge in lemming population was considered separately from the instant decrease when they commit
suicide. Killing off lemmings in fear of destruction of their food sources could
lead to the extinction of the lemmings. Feedback became crucial to the development of family therapy when families were observed together over time and a
pattern was observed whereby there was always one member with a problem,
but the patient and the problem would change. Looking at this long-term negative feedback process, maintaining one sick person, with intervals of positive
feedback, changing member, changing condition, gives a fuller picture of the
family's dynamics. A nonsystems view might tend to attack single manifest
conditions like failing in school, setting a positive feedback process in motion.
However, if the accompanying negative feedback process is not considered, the
intervention may mean that one child improves at school while another becomes anorexic.

In terms of theory, feedback is a crucial buttress of the basic orientation of systems theory as nonassumptive. By looking at the patterns as patterns with no inherent correctness or appropriateness, it is possible to move away from blaming and attempt to get inside the cultural specificity of a context, and in so doing design more fitting models.

In research strategies this points to the need to delay closure until there is sufficient information to see how the long-term positive and negative feedback processes fit the overall pattern of events in a context. Practically this means observing linked sequences of action, reaction, and counter reaction and expanding the time frame until patterns are observed repeating. More immediately, feedback can be used to critique quick-fix solutions to complex problems. Recalling my earlier discussion in Chapter 2, has the massive publicity given to cross-border shopping from southern Ontario, Canada, to Buffalo, New York, led to the increase in this practice and the legalizing of Sunday shopping in Ontario? Will legalizing Sunday shopping in Ontario ultimately increase cross-border shopping even more as Canadian retailers are forced to increase prices in order to compensate for the increased costs of staying open another day each week? Will this process mean that U.S.-based companies operating in Canada increase their market share and drive Canadian companies out of business?

In essence feedback adds form to the systems basic: everything is related to everything. The definition of a system of two or more interrelated parts, such that changing one changes all, gives rise to considering how change occurs. Feedback, positive and negative, elaborates patterns of change and nonchange and in so doing provides a language for looking for ongoing processes in systems.

EQUIFINALITY AND MULTIFINALITY

*When acting on a system, you can get the same result from
a variety of stimuli (equifinality) or a variety of results
from the same stimuli (multifinality).*

Why is it that no matter how hard you try you end up fighting with your parents every time they visit?

Why is it that despite stated efforts to improve the standard of living, illiteracy and food bank dependency are increasing?

Equifinality and multifinality are concepts that provide a means for investigating these questions. Together they express the idea that when you act on a system of interrelated parts, you cannot gauge the effects based on knowledge of the input alone. In order to understand the ensuing events, you must have

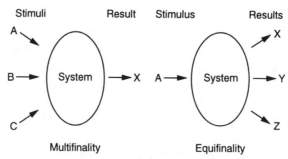

Figure 2 Equifinality and multifinality. From "Conceptualizing contextual emotion: The grounds for 'supra-rationality'," by B. G. Hanson, 1991, *Diogenes*, Fall (156), p. 43. Reprinted with permission.

knowledge of the system as well. You must understand the emotional loading of a parent–child relationship before you can try to change it. An intervention of this tendency may exacerbate the situation. If you want to reduce poverty, you must understand how elements of the social context, like racism and sexism, contribute to escalating the proportion of people living below the poverty line.

Equifinality captures the idea that when you act on a system, a number of different stimuli can lead to the same result. "Equi" plus "final," means "same end." Multifinality refers to the idea that you can get a number of different results from the same stimuli. "Multi" plus "final," means "many ends."

The figure above illustrates the property of systems of equi- and multifinality. The key message is to attend to the overall pattern in time to figure out what the ultimate result or results from specific stimulus or stimuli are. It becomes a crucial part of a wholes approach in that it provides a frame for beginning the process of intervention by giving form to the popular notion of side effects. Furthermore, because time is so inextricably linked to a notion of equi- or multifinality, there is a means to move models of potential effects, intended and unintended, through extended time frames.

These concepts are "de rigueur" to my recent ideas on "The Myth of the Biological Time Clock" and "Cardiology and Castration." In "Myth" I look at how the belief in the existence of a biological time clock in a female body aging past 35 has serious negative effects on fertility outcomes and has created statistics that confirm the myth. In so doing the myth has been magnified in equifinal fashion. Things like reproductive and neonatal technology, increasing cesarean section rates, and antifeminist backlash (Faludi, 1991) have all worked in concert in the broader social context to ingrain and solidify the myth of a biological time clock, while scientific evidence that it is a myth is readily available. I use the notion of equifinality to frame this process as one where, in a social context pervaded by sexism, the creation and maintenance of a myth of a biological time clock is predictable. All evidence, even if contradictory, leads to the same sexist conclusion.

In "Cardiology and Castration" I look at how the same prevailing sexist attitudes have led in multifinal fashion to the proliferation and promotion of cancer and various modes of treatment for women's health. A single stimulus is the ideology that equates gender with sex—the social construction of woman and man is a direct outgrowth of the biological attributes of female and male. I have discussed the inappropriateness of this equation in the section on unit. The equation is inappropriate both theoretically and practically as it wanders directly into the realm of health as a sex-based modality for intervention that has over-laid artifacts of sex onto the social construct of gender.

At the beginning of the 1900s, forays into the study of cancer showed that women got cancer more often than men and more so after age 50 (Hoffman, 1915). It was thus hypothesized that loss of estrogen causes cancer. Estrogen supplements were prescribed. As time went on and detection techniques improved, women under 50 got cancer. Then it was concluded, it must be too much estrogen. In 1966 a Nobel Prize was given to someone for the theory of a hormone connection to cancer (American Cancer Society, 1967). In the late 1970s this theory was given close scrutiny and was found to be questionable, with the best evidence being of estrogen supplements showing a tendency to promote cancer (Meakin, 1979). The overlay of sex on gender, in this case female/hormones, wandered into the treatment of men as well as women. Hysterectomies have been used to treat cancer even in cases where the cancer is outside the genitourinary tract. In multifinal fashion the sexist overlay on health has led to a variety of outcomes in the area of cancer research, promotion, and treatment.

In relative fashion it is possible to consider that there may be equifinal or multifinal results when acting on a system. Gauging that is likely under which circumstances with which systems becomes the target of analysis. This mode of analysis is most crucial in situations where interventions, attempts to change, are the goal. Equifinality points out that the ultimate effects of an action may in fact not change the targeted situation at all in the long run, and may even exacerbate that situation. Multifinality points out that the intended result of an action may have a host of unintended offshoots and may cause more new problems than the original problem.

As with all concepts of a wholes approach, there is no prescriptive direction in the concepts themselves. Rather, they are intended to give a form and language for analysis. The content of the patterns that lead to equifinal or multifinal processes may thus involve looking at various elements of assumed patterns in targeted context.

Equifinality comes through as an important organizing concept in the consideration of mental illness in family contexts. The lingering images of schizophrenia in families in Laing and Esterson's *Sanity, Madness and the Family* (1964) provide haunting portraits of situations where a child's behavior is all interpreted into a frame of illness. As the child enters adolescence, changes like making friends, seeking independence, sexual awakening, religious questioning, change in dress, and so on, become threatening. These multiple changes or stimuli are all funnelled into maintenance of the idea that the child is dependent and incapable. When this definition is challenged by evidence such as external praise or competence, control is exerted like not letting the teenager go out on dates. Or, behavior may be tolerated but considered evidence of mental illness: being promiscuous, manically devoted to the Bible, or other negative interpretations. In total, a whole array of stimuli are directed at the same result—the incapability of the child—setting a perpetual dependence, or perpetual childhood, in motion.

An organizational level process that shows equifinality (many things leading to a single result) is the various stimuli that lead to increases in the overall operating budget for running a college or university. Lowering student enrollment leads to increased student enrollment. Restricting the availability of new entrance spots at a university has increased the value of education such that demand for course enrollment for students already in stream increases and encourages students to take more degrees while they can. Trying to decrease the number of faculty leads to a situation where faculty are developing burgeoning levels of credentials, which allow them to make higher salary demands. Trying to encourage early retirement for high salary faculty prompts more people to resist retirement longer. Increasing class sizes encourages faculty to go into administrative positions that buy out their teaching responsibilities. Cost-cutting pressure in one country will encourage faculty with the best credentials and highest research profiles to go to jobs in other countries where they have more support for their research and teaching. Either these faculty are not replaced at all or their jobs are filled with faculty with less credentials. The university has trouble attracting grants for research or getting public support.

A relevant 20th century policy example of multifinality is the process that ensued with the advent of Prohibition. A single act or stimuli led to a variety of unanticipated results, some of which were the obverse of the intended goal, eliminating alcohol consumption. With the rise of the temperance movement and the formation of the Women's Christian Temperance Union, Prohibition was put into place. This immediately raised the levels of profits to be made in the illegal making and selling of liquor. Black markets for selling liquor sprang up quickly, doing business at prices greatly increased over the previous legal prices. Crime syndicates arose in the competition for this now highly profitable market. One of the more famous crime figures was Al Capone, whose demise is chronicled in the movie *The Untouchables*. Speakeasies, bathtub gin, and moonshine proliferated. Smuggling exports from non-Prohibition countries became profitable. Side effects like blindness resulting from improper liquor making techniques co-emerged. As we near the close of the 20th century, alcohol consumption is widespread through all sectors of the population in North America. In sum, the multifinal process that ensued after the imposition of Prohibition led to a variety of unanticipated results.

Equifinality and multifinality are extensions of the systems basis that change in one part changes all parts. They provide images of patterns in changes and whether parts change or stay the same. Equifinality crops up in the pioneering work of von Bertalanffy (1968), although in his usage it seems to rely on the notion of using equifinality to explain the goal-directed nature of systems. This derives from observations in biology that it is possible to dissect embryos into pieces, giving the example of sea urchins, and develop a whole organism from each piece (von Bertalanffy, 1975). I accept the notion of equifinality in the sense of various inputs leading to the same result, but discard this as a necessarily goal-directed process. I argue that the concept of goal-directed nature is assumptive and as such detracts from the brand of systems theory I present in terms of a wholes approach. Goal-directed nature can be tied to the kind of status quo conservative ideology that runs through later applications of systems theory in the realm of structural functionalism. I do not accept this type of extension as inherent to a general systems theory approach in that it implies progress and consensus. I prefer, because of this, to discard it.

Multifinality is an extension of the idea of equifinality that I learned from Norman W. Bell at the University of Toronto and have not been able to find in systems writing. It extends the principle of equifinality. If systems have emergent wholes not witnessed on the level of individual components, then any number of stimuli can lead to the same result: equifinality. It is a corollary that any single stimulus can lead to a number of different results, multifinality. This principle is seen in recent uses of undifferentiated human fetal tissue which, if taken at an early point, can develop into any number of types of human cells. Any tissue transplanted into recipient brains or livers becomes brain or liver tissue. This is now being used to treat Parkinson's disease and is raising issues about abortion and the use of fetal tissue.

Theory is directed by equifinality and multifinality to a more sophisticated view of what changes and what stays the same. Positive and negative feedback provide a focus on change and nonchange. Equifinality and multifinality allow differentiating feedback processes over time and separating out forms of change and new emergent properties. They add a sense of prediction in terms of stimuli and result, which frame initial attention to the fundamental process of feedback. Equifinality and multifinality are thus qualifications and extensions of the basic notions in feedback. While positive and negative feedback give raw sensitivity to interactive or cybernetic, as opposed to linear causality, equifinality and multifinality allow looking for the emergent results of feedback processes.

The major message for research and accompanying intervention is to focus simultaneously on time and process. Equifinal and multifinal results mean going into a time frame that looks long term at what the results of any action may be. I read about initial attempts to increase the population of a rare form of blue jay. At first people tried building mass numbers of nesting sites. This was unsuccessful because although the blue jays had more chance to nest and reproduce, so did the insects that preyed on their eggs. The first attempts may have even decreased the blue jay population (Darling & Thomson-Delaney, 1992). Above all, caution is advised until enough is known about the characteristics of the system of interest. This owes to the fact that intervention naive of systems properties for co-emergence may do precisely the obverse of what is intended and create new problems that are worse than the initial target problems. The examples of rent control and Prohibition demonstrate this need for caution and attention to the system as a whole rather than as merely the sum of its parts.

Personal experiences with repetitive painful romances, escalating violence, body weight, substance abuse in a loved one, or deteriorating financial security can bring to mind the messages of equifinality and multifinality. It is possible to question what patterns in one's own system of intimate relations lead to cyclic repetitive results despite varying intentions to change and break the cycle. How may attempts to break the cycle have accelerated it and brought about new problems?

PART TWO

CHARACTERISTICS

Characteristics are properties that serve to reveal or distinguish,
in this case particular features of human systems.

In Part One of this book I outlined basic concepts that go into a wholes or general systems theory approach. Part Two picks up on those concepts and elaborates possible characteristics of human systems that can be added to a wholes approach. This should be read as a "may contain" list.

I use three sets of assumptions about humans, content, communication, and emotion, each treated in a separate chapter, to flesh out a wholes model of human group behavior. The purpose in this presentation is to begin adding specific form and substance to the more abstract notions of a systems approach. The concepts we have dealt with thus far can be applied to any kind of system: spouses, marketing teams, government agencies, amoebas, stereos, computers, lakes, planets, fires, ant colonies, and so on. They have been derived and explicated largely for audiences in the physical and technical sciences like biology, physics, engineering, and mathematics. Because of this, the basics of a wholes approach have often been presented in the language and modes of thinking specific to those types of disciplines.

Where systems theory has been applied previously in the realm of the social sciences, its predominant focus has been on a very specific brand of systems theory. There are two main thrusts in this area: structural functionalism and hierarchical systems.

Structural functionalism, often referred to as consensus theory, picks up on the systems basis of nonsummativity. It adds assumptive notions like function (parts for the good of whole) and social facts—wholes as external, and therefore amenable to logical positivist analysis. An organismic analogy is applied to liken social systems to biological systems and attempt to show that function and survival are natural processes of specialization based on inherent capabilities. The only requisite for defining structural functionalism as a systems approach is using nonsummativity as a point of departure, which it does. However, all the assumptive additions like organismic analogy, consensus, function, and social facts are uniquely functionalist. None is inherent to a general systems theory approach.

The other strain of thinking about systems theory in the social sciences has been the hierarchical models of authors like Buckley (1967b), Luhmann (1982), and Sorokin (1957). Again these representations take nonsummativity as a point of departure and are therefore legitimately defined as systems theories. From there they add the sociological assumption of society and begin to define elaborate models of hierarchical levels of society. The addition of a society assumption with the implied notion of hierarchy is uniquely the choice of these authors coming from a sociological approach.

There are alternative systems approaches to human systems, one of which I present here. My version of a general systems theory, the wholes approach, presents a viable alternative to both of these strains of thinking by going back to the basic concepts I outlined in the first part of the book and adding a set of assumptions regarding characteristics in the social sciences that have never been integrated before. By going through each of the assumptive heritages in turn—subjectivity as a question of content, dual communication, and a suprarational model of emotion within the frame of a wholes approach—a new means of viewing human group phenomena co-emerges.

The importance of this new form of systems approach lies in seeing that the groundbreaking insights of the basis of a wholes approach have not been fully utilized in the social sciences. It is possible to argue that this lack of use can be traced to problems in the disciplines of social sciences themselves rather than problems with general systems theory. In the case of functionalist applications, the assumption of consensus or status quo ideology has limited its insights to that belief box. There is no escaping beyond the parameters that define it in the first place. Either you believe in the rightness of the right or you do not.

While legitimate, this presents no means of transforming the classic left/right consensus/conflict antinomy: two contradictory but equally valid propositions. Moving to other forms of assumptions, like human subjectivity, communication as a complex of verbal and nonverbal signals, and emotion as a central human characteristic, is more useful. Debate on these assumptions about human group characteristics may ultimately fall into the same paradoxical impasse as has the left/right dichotomy. But for the moment they may provide novel paths to explore because they are less territorialized and seem to cut across the assumptive bases of more conventional schools of thought.

The notion of hierarchy is not necessary for a wholes approach and is as restrictive as is the consensus belief box. Beginning with the assumption of society has predisposed an irreconcilable debate about levels. By first assuming the hierarchical structure of society as a series of levels and then trying to analyze away these defining boundaries, a paradox is set up. We see society as levels. Let us talk about resolving the micro/macro level debate. To begin with level is to be trapped by level.

To transcend this trap is to leave the assumption of hierarchy aside. It is possible to reframe the issue in terms of causality, rather than level, and focus instead on determinacy as the question (Hanson, 1994b). In this manner a wholes approach provides a means of escape from the prescriptive boxes of level by moving instead to a cybernetic model of causality. It is possible to see that the drive to seat cause or determinacy in parts such as levels is itself an irreconcilable dilemma. There is no means of resolve when the debate itself is defined in terms of separation of parts into levels. Into the fray, a cybernetic or feedback model of causality throws a means of escape, by taking away the problematic separation that spawned the debate in the first place. It is somewhat like two children fighting over a box of crayons. A parent can shift attention to a different form of task, such as baking, that does not require an either/or resolution with the crayons. In the same manner a wholes approach shifts attention from causes to patterns of events over time, feedback processes.

A wholes approach is thus situated in a position to transcend two classic antinomies of modeling in the social sciences: the left/right and micro/macro debates. To give a specific form to this potential, I offer one possible alternative on three assumptive axes: content, communication, and emotion. In so doing I hope to give additional substance to a wholes approach for the social sciences. It is worthwhile to keep in mind throughout this presentation, however, that there is no reason these axes cannot be transported into other areas of inquiry. I hope and suspect that they will.

Ever since Darwin there has been a great deal of effort put into the question of how the human being relates to the variety of species and physical phenomena that fall subject to analysis. How are humans different from other creatures, the tides, and computers? Are they different at all? This question has often taken on a religious tone depending on the context in which it has been asked. The wholes approach provides a pan-disciplinary, and because of this, pan-phenomena language. As this language is worked with and applied, it is possible to begin adding fuel to questions about humanness—what it is and is not. At the same time it is possible to re-examine questions about phenomena previously considered discrete. Can dolphins communicate? What is intelligence and can it be synthesized? Where does spirituality lie? Is there a parallel between the explosiveness and unpredictability of human relationships and the co-emergence of nonsummative results, like computer viruses?

In this manner, by beginning from the social sciences and looking at human groups using a wholes approach, it may be possible to spur on thinking in the physical and technical sciences, which spawned systems thinking. My perception of previous problems in making these connections to the benefit of both realms has led me to believe that "discipline-centrism" has led to unnecessary distrust and disrespect. The importance of finding ways to begin a dialogue on a common ground is tied to the increasingly urgent need for attention to ways in which emotion, ideology, competition, and creativity come into play in global patterns of conflict and environmental degradation. So to begin the path of determining the characteristics of human systems is to try a fresh approach to problems that are known but are not resolvable within current frames of scholarly reference.

Chapter 5

Content

Content refers to co-emergent meaning in context.

The previous discussions have all been grounded in a notion of context—emergent wholes that are the focus of analysis. This chapter begins the process of outlining the content of wholes. The content and context concept allows separation of the theoretical imperative of nonsummativity from the elements that flesh out a theory of a particular emergent whole. By way of analogy, think for a moment of a cartoon. Context is the justification for creating the "bubbles" that appear above characters. Content speaks to that with which the bubbles are filled.

My discussion of content in this chapter is directed to a notion of human subjective capabilities. I am directing myself to the processes whereby humans in groups develop categories and language and how they use such symbolic attachments in the acting out of their lives. This discussion can take place in terms of varying contexts of origin for such contents. As part two goes on, you will see that content becomes a specific type of output that is driven by other processes of emotion and communication. The content itself becomes diagnostic of higher order characteristics of human systems. The content of a degrading term will be tied to contents available in a context. However, the patterns that lead to degradation are tied to patterns in higher order properties, most centrally emotion.

A content–context conceptualization brings a wholes approach closer to applications with human systems by moving away from a rational overlay. This is a more fitting use of a general systems theory approach. By moving to a view of nonsummative emotional characteristics, it is possible to move away from the implicit linear grounding of a model of human rationality. So as I discuss the areas of meaning, parallogic, realities, and dual communication, it must be kept in mind that these are initial steps toward what I model as the central feature of human groups: emotion.

The business of content acquisition can be seen as a rational process, in the sense of direct connections. The question of when, or in which context, a particular content is used is one of explosive and dampening co-emergent properties of human systems. Take the example of a derogatory sexist word. Such language is part of a wider context that is based in, and reinforces, sexist ideology. People learn the wide array of possible sexist words as they interact with others, as well as the particularly offensive selections in a given context, for instance, an intimate relationship. Content means both acquiring that range and learning the most specifically effective term for a context of reference. When a person actually uses the term will be driven by the emotional patterns of the context. A person may know the derogatory terms X, Y, and Z are appropriate ways to degrade a woman. They will also learn which of the three upsets and hurts this particular woman the most. When "Y" comes out at this woman, it will be driven by the context patterns, say during a heated argument or in response to the man's feeling threatened when she got a good grade or a raise.

In the case of an organization that is trying to sell something like dolls, there may be a known content of products (male, female, talking, wetting, hard, soft), but the question of which contents work at what time is a co-emergent nonrational phenomenon. Several years ago the "Cabbage Patch" dolls exemplified this notion. Was there some rational known formula for explaining the massive demand for these dolls? If so, why didn't any of the competing alternatives that tried to break down and copy the formula succeed? The message is that joint contextual "suprarationality," as we will come to know it in Chapter 6, means that outcomes are not predictable based on knowledge of content alone. The world of marketing is replete with examples of inexplicable fad buying, such as Hoola Hoops, Pet Rocks, and more recently the stuffed animal halves that stick out of people's car trunks or the whole stuffed animals that stick onto car windows with suction cups.

In terms of policy, there is the example of the boom and bust economies of the 1980s and 1990s and how they are fed by the content of policy and the emotional reactivity of contexts. On the one hand we have consistent policies like keeping interest rates high in order to quell inflation. This content was available for years. Why all of a sudden have we seen a rapid downward spiral? The content of high interest rates has been blamed in the frame of linear causality. Explanation based on this content, a rational linear frame alone, should mean that lowering interest rates will have the reverse effect: it will begin and maintain an upward surge. I offer that neither the question of why a downward trend exists at a certain point, nor why no upward trend is evident now, can be explained effectively by a pure content or rational model. It is necessary to combine diagnosis of content with the driving context characteristic of emotion in order to capture this phenomena. Consumer faith, entrepreneur confidence, national pride, and depression are all emotional terms that emerge in explanations of market trends, yet their intuitive application and human emotional context is not modeled.

CONTENT AND CONTEXT: WHY ONE AND NOT ANOTHER?

Looking at emergent wholes offers a way of explaining why the same conditions don't correlate to the same events.

The central point to the discussion of content is that the issue of content is simultaneously an issue of context. The jumping board of nonsummativity, context, when carried into the realm of human group behavior, suggests the addition of a construct of meaning when the assumption is taken that humans have subjective capabilities. Emotion takes this conception further by differentiating which available meanings or contents play out or not, and in which contexts.

The main contribution of the conceptual separation of content and context is to show how the implicit epistemological overlay of hierarchy and linear causality in the study of human groups can be critiqued using a wholes approach. The alternative of cybernetic cause provides a means of transcending the failure of conventional theories in behavioral science to explain individual events. While average tendencies in populations of like conditions can be explained, predictions of the specific remain elusive. It is not possible to explain why, under like structural conditions, Jim Doe beats his spouse while John Doe does not. Models that hone in on the content of a cultural context alone are destined to be limited to the rational and linear suppositions that ground the explanation.

To separate the content of the general from the context of the particular is to go beyond this limitation. It is possible to seat content in a context, then look for the characteristics of this context that lead to the use of a content. The flexibility provided by a wholes approach may appear as a question of level in the sense that it is possible to avoid the trap of assuming structural reproduction at all levels of the system. I argue that this is peripheral to the more central feature of moving to a cybernetic model of causality that renders the level issue moot.

Content is co-emergent and therefore does not need to be seated in any fixed causal position. Emotion as an overriding characteristic of human groups renders the causal position of content secondary. While watching for contents in process may tell us about the system, like the dye in an angiogram or a barium enema, it is not the system. Systems are co-emergent contexts with nonsummative properties beyond any single content component.

To research within the content–context separation is to begin mapping out patterns of the phenomena that can allow content variables to be considered as diagnostic rather than deterministic of the context of interest. It is thus possible to retain familiar contents like age, gender, class, and race, while framing their contributions in a nonconventional mode.

This has come out in my own work in terms of modeling the "patienting" process in mental illness (Hanson, 1994a, 1994c, 1994d). I elaborate a pattern in intimate contexts that is more, and conversely less, likely to be correlated with the process of defining a family member as sick. A content–context separation enters by arguing that while the process of defining a patient in intimacy is a characteristic of that context, the process of patienting is coded into age and gender categories through contact with the clinical realm.

A move by intimates to "patient" in response to emotional distress may be mediated by outside contact, which enters into the process of determining which member becomes and remains identified as a patient, while the distress is a feature of the intimate context as a whole. Over time the person who is a patient may change and the illness label may change, but the emotional distress lingers. A family may respond to emotional distress by considering the problem to be an aged woman, the mother. If the clinician does not accept this explanation, then another problem may be sought, the teenage daughter. If this new explanation is not supported, there may be a move to the teenage son. In sum the clinician may be prepared to read only specific age–gender pairings in individuals, while the impetus to seek help derives from the intimate context as a whole. It will project as a series of individual illnesses in age and gender categories over time. This pattern of projections tells us both about the pervasiveness of the emotional distress in a family context as well as the tendency for illness labels to follow age and sex content in a social context where ageist and sexist ideology co-emerge.

Perhaps it is possible to begin thinking about emotional characteristics of contexts that fuel a general pattern of content seeking in the form of reductionist categories. Imagine yourself driving along the road. A car cuts you off and nearly causes an accident. As you look at the driver is there an instant angry urge to reduce this person to some age, gender, or racial category. Does that content have any rational relation to something that would explain the behavior? Or does it co-emerge in the process of an emotional reaction to subjugate or hurt? Content is thus read onto the emotional context.

MEANING

People act based not on objects, but rather
on the meaning objects have for them.

This is the basis of a consideration of meaning as a characteristic of human groups in general and for my consideration of human groups as systems or wholes. This notion picks up on the idea that humans are meaning-making, in the sense that they have the capacity to create, reflect, and interpret their worlds of experience. While it may be possible to think about a world of objective existence for things like chairs and trees, the human experience is one of making meaning for such objects.

Meaning models human beings as reflective and creative in the sense of being able to refract and interpret any given objective stimuli. This is in direct contradiction to the so-called "black box" view that models humans as simple stimulus–response, input–output relays, much the same as pigeons or rats.

These stances, as illustrated in Figure 3, differ in terms of the efficacy and capabilities they attribute to human beings. Do humans add to and modify what they perceive? Or, do they merely react without alteration? The fundamental position of a consideration of meaning in human groups is the former: Humans interpret and create a world of meaning that mediates all behavior.

After considering a model of human beings as meaning-making, it is possible to move on to consider the hows and kinds of meaning construction. The second element of the stance is that meaning co-emerges in a concert production between human beings. The kinds of meanings that are made or constructed will thus be mediated by the groups in which they arise and the environments in which the process takes place. For example, Aboriginal people living in the far north and skiers develop a shared set of meanings for snow that arises uniquely to those groups. Both the hunter and the cross-country skier need to have a variety of symbols or meanings to describe different types of

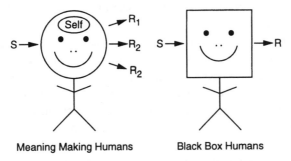

Meaning Making Humans   Black Box Humans

Figure 3   The concept of human meaning making.

snow. In the case of skiing, expressions like "corn," "powder," "boilerplate," "manmade," "corduroy," and so on, are used to describe different types of snow that affect ski waxing and the techniques used to ski. A city dweller who never skis may only learn one symbol, "snow," to capture all the varieties because this array of differentiation is not relevant to his or her shared experience. It all has to be shoveled! What this shows us is that human groups have the capability of developing shared meanings, symbols, or language, which may be unique to the experiences of any given context.

Take the example of two people establishing an intimate relationship. As time goes on they meet each others' families. Imagine the scene at the dinner table when the newcomer inadvertently hits upon THE SUBJECT that nobody mentions. In my family it was fleas. Or the trouble may have to do with assimilating the patterns of food passing, language (even if the formal language is common), speaking order, and so on. A friend told me that her family always started dinner precisely at ten to six, and at six o'clock the radio went on and everyone had to be quiet so father could listen to some radio show. If a newcomer were to speak up during the program, they would be severely chastised. As more dinners are attended the newcomer will learn the shared symbols and be able to participate in the context.

In organizational contexts examples abound of shared meanings unique to a group that have no inherent meaning outside the group. Recently a friend began selling cars and learned that the expression for a potential customer who walks into the showroom is "up," as in, "It's your up." In the tourist industry of the Canadian Rockies the term "Gorbie" is used to refer to tacky tourists. I remember the expression, "the English are a people separated by a common language." If one travels to various contexts where English is the main language, the relevance of context-specific meanings and symbols becomes apparent. Another Canadian friend was renting an apartment in the United States and had trouble asking about "hydro," the Canadian reference to utilities such as natural gas and electricity. Finally the rental agent said "Do you mean power?" I, living in New Jersey on sabbatical, had to learn that what I knew as a "washroom" is a "restroom." In the United Kingdom it is "the loo," a "lorry" is a truck, the "boot" is the car trunk, one "rings" rather than calls someone, and "crisps" are potato chips. Shared meaning sets develop in cultures as well as in intimacy.

Policy disasters have occurred frequently when the context-specific nature of meanings has not been considered. My example of attempts to limit population growth from the first part of this book is also relevant here. These efforts in developing nations showed problems arising from ignorance of context as birth control technology and education, which worked nicely in the middle and upper class of industrialized nations, had no effect. It was not until analysis that took context into account was done that it was learned that birth control was an irrelevant concept because people in impoverished circumstances had no desire to limit births. Children, while an economic liability in the middle and upper classes of industrialized nations, are an economic asset in the lower classes or in developing nations.

The message in meaning is that to assume direct cause and effect relationships when acting on human systems is erroneous. This is a basic suggestion of cybernetic causality, but an observation that derives from a number of other lines of thought. Meaning provides the characteristic of human systems that enables explanation of why birth control works differently in a posh suburb of London than it does in the slums of New York or the rainforests of South America. A model of biochemical reactions of female physiology to oral contraceptives is not useful universally when some women want to take them while others do not.

The two principal lines of thought that can be woven into a wholes approach to meaning are symbolic interactionism (Blumer, 1969; Goffman, 1961) and constructivist thought (von Glasersfeld, 1984). Though they have different heritages, their basic stance is the same: people act based not on objects but rather on the meaning objects have for them. Where the two schools differ is in terms of focus; the small group in the case of symbolic interaction and the broader social context in the case of constructivism. This difference is not particularly relevant within a systems approach in that the question of level, which underpins these conceptions, is superseded by the move to cybernetic causality. What is relevant is the common focus on the importance of shared group meanings. In discussing the concept of parallogic in the next section, it is possible to see how this notion of context specificity of meaning tied to a notion of context can be set into motion with a concept of process to explain events like judgment of appropriateness, typified by the question of mental illness.

Though the deriving traditions of symbolic interactionism and constructivism may not have phrased it this way, it is possible to use the characteristic of meaning to direct focus to contexts. It is possible to begin thinking theoretically about a notion of a defined context, such as intimate relations, and look for how meaning sets specific to that context interphase with meaning sets of other contexts, such as a cultural context, in the co-emergent process of events of interest. In this manner it is possible to look at how the available symbols of gender, race, and class are used within the frame of meanings of a particular context. This allows us to explore a problematic to structural analysis. Why one and not another under like structural conditions?

Researchers need to be constantly aware that the assumption that the meanings of the researcher are the same as the meanings of the researched may be, or even always is, erroneous. This necessitates a contextual view of not just research subjects but research staff as well (Hanson, in press-a). If we accept a model of human subjectivity, meaning-making, we must also accept that the subjective processes of social construction are inherent to the process of research design, data collection, and analysis. This adds a metalevel analysis to the question of research methods as we move to consider theoretically what thinking of researchers as subjective humans means. In my own work this has spawned analysis of the coding context and how the feelings and impressions of researchers can be utilized as part and parcel of the phenomena of interest (Hanson, in press-b).

In practical terms, the characteristic of meaning points out that problems of adjustment to new situations or known situations where meaning is not shared can be framed in terms of context-specific differences rather than individual failings. A person can begin to see that the trouble she has in excelling in the context of meaning that she does not share may derive from the fact that the necessary symbols are known better by the men who control the meaning context. In the corporate world the expression "glass ceiling" has arisen to capture the observation that women seem to be admitted to the lower levels of the professional ladder but are prevented from getting to the top. A salient part of this process is the symbol sets that do not equate the object of "women" with the meaning "executive" and derive from contexts of the experience of men. Expressions like "end run," "punt," "let's tee it up and see where it flies," and so on, which derive from male-dominated sports and wander into the lingo of the boardroom, may put women who do not share the meaning context at a disadvantage for understanding and making themselves understood.

PARALLOGIC

*Parallogic captures the notion that because meaning is specific
to context, systems of logic are parallel.*

"To begin with," said the Cat, "a dog's not mad. You grant me that?"
"I suppose so," said Alice.
"Well, then," the Cat went on, "you see a dog growls when it's angry, and wags its tail when it's pleased. Now I growl when I'm pleased, and wag my tail when I'm angry. Therefore I'm mad." (Carroll, 1865/1981, pp. 47–48)

It is possible to take the idea of meaning as a subjective creation of human groups and join it to a concept of context, emergent wholes in groups of two or more parts. This makes it possible to model systems of logic as parallel in the sense of being lines that never meet. This contradicts the conventional stance of seeing logic as a universal from which various paths deviate.

While reality may be objective, meaning is subjective, and therefore context specific. Judging any given behavior as appropriate or inappropriate, sane or insane, needs to be done relative to its native context, else we risk the Cat's classification errors. In human contexts this points to the need to be aware, when judgments are being made, of the context of the judge and that of the persons being judged.

The parallogical message is that by linking the suggestions of a concept of meaning, with its roots in symbolic interactionism and constructivism, to a wholes notion of context via nonsummativity, it is possible to transcend a view of universal logic or rationality. The reference point for logic, rationality, or sanity becomes moot, and reference points become the focus. This ties in with the post-modernist idea that ". . . an absolute point is no longer assumed to be available to legitimize truth and order" (Murphy, 1988, p. 95). A parallogical view offers that while there is no single point, there are *points*.

As such it is possible to shift thinking about legitimacy, be it in terms of people who come to be defined as mentally ill or in cultures where race and gender enter into judgments. It is possible to use the image of a parallogical view to encourage sensitivity to native context as a precursor to judgment. The departure of this model from conventional universal views can be shown by contrasting a parallogical view with the conventional "contralogical" view in Figure 4.

Here we see that the degree of separation between two systems of logic may be equal, but judging this gap as normal or abnormal depends on whether the separation is judged to be difference or deviation. Thus the parallogical imperative is to situate any event in its native context before judging it, rather than assuming any gap between the observer's system and logic and that of what is being judged as illogical.

It seems this is an important principle in situations of judgment where native

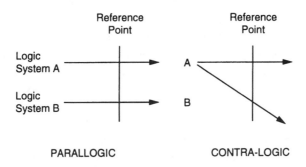

Figure 4 Parallogic. From "Parallogic: As mind meets context," by B. G. Hanson, 1989, *Diogenes*, Fall (147), p. 81. Reprinted with permission.

awareness of meaning is prone to gaps between the judge and those who are judged. This is particularly relevant to situations such as those where this is difference between the age, gender, race, or class of assessors relative to those being assessed.

One of my favorite examples of this principle in intimate relations is the book *The Stone Angel* by Margaret Laurence (1978), in which unfolds the story of Hagar, an aged woman in the Canadian Prairies who is living with her son and daughter-in-law as her health deteriorates. The story is replete with examples in which the middle generation cannot understand what Hagar's actions mean, nor can Hagar understand their actions because they do not share context. "Danish Modern, the world is full of mysteries, and I will not ask. Wouldn't she love to think me ignorant, wouldn't she just" (p. 56). These actions are constantly interpreted by the son and daughter-in-law as evidence of illness, uncooperativeness, and memory gaps. This leads to considerable distress for all members of the household as Hagar and her daughter-in-law, Doris, reinforce a pattern of mutual resentment, leading to lingering pain and downward-spiraling self-esteem. Taking a parallogical view in this instance allows the reader to see how so much of Hagar's behavior was not insane or forgetful, but rather these were attempts to cover up feelings of bereavement, inefficacy, and insecurity. In a real-life relationship, an effort at giving mutual awareness of each others' contexts of meaning to both Hagar and Doris might have reduced the pain of the situation.

In terms of health care, it is possible to think about the case of PMS (premenstrual syndrome). For a long time women had been reporting certain symptoms—pain, discomfort, irritability, and bloating for the two weeks prior to the onset of menstruation. These phenomena reported to a medical profession dominated by men were dismissed as "being all in their heads" and thus, non-problems. More recently, as research was focused on the issue, it became apparent that these symptoms were in fact common experiences for the majority of women and that they were accompanied by detectable biological changes in female physiology. I would phrase this change as resulting from a parallogical shift in which the native context of women was given inherent legitimacy by the medical profession and then investigated as such. In contrast, the original medical stance to dismiss these reports as nonsensical or illegitimate resulted from a contralogical view whereby the assessors' own context of logic was taken as the universal.

What has changed here via a parallogical shift is that women have created a context in which their concerns can be voiced, heard, and acted upon. However, it can be argued that little has changed outside this new context of women's health and self-support. To wit, in the broader context of conventional medicine, there have been attempts to define PMS as a psychiatric condition that, given that the majority of women have symptoms of PMS, would by implication define being a woman as a psychiatric condition. This makes a parallogical view crucial in order to show that all judgments are relative to their context. The nature of a judgment or recommendation therefore depends on that context.

Perhaps a parallogical view can frame discussions and problems that have arisen over the past few years in trying to establish a Canadian constitution. The history of this process is replete with examples of how focus on the content of one group as the assumed universal has led to problems with other contexts of meaning and their accompanying logic. Problems with one version of the new constitution prompted the Canadian Prime Minister to call a private meeting of the provincial premiers at his weekend retreat at Meech Lake. This resulted in the "Meech Lake Accord," which had a "distinct society" clause that recognized the particular meaning content of Quebec. It did not, however, take into account the fact that by giving centrality to one context many others were now rendered contralogical. Consequently the context-specific nature of other contents like women, First Nations members, and the other provinces, was now deviant and therefore unrecognized. This led to the voting down of the accord by one province and the occupation of a commuter bridge into Montreal by First Nations groups. Since then a parallogical stance seems to have emerged as members of parliament went across Canada trying to get a feel for the parallogics that make up Canada. This issue continues to be debated. It returned to a private debate with Quebec refusing to participate without veto power, in essence defining a contralogical view that is Quebec-centric. More recently, in the last federal election a federal party centered in Quebec won a sizable number of seats, and an election to poll desires for Quebec separation is in the offing.

This is also seen in the U.S. debates about health care reform. Doctors, insurance companies, political interest groups, and patients have very different contexts in which to view the issue. Doctors and insurance companies may be concerned with protecting a lucrative financial situation. Right-wing groups may see extending health care to the fullest possible proportion of the population as just another form of welfare, and suggest contrarily that it would be better to get people out working and paying for it personally. Left-wing intellectuals praise universal health care as a step toward social justice and equality. Wealthy patients may fear erosion of the quality of health care they are able to afford as the system is extended to cover most Americans. Poor patients hail it as a godsend that will alleviate one of their greatest fears: that they or someone they love will fall ill and they will not be able to afford the treatment needed to help them get well. An understanding of the situation is relative to each of these contexts. Consequently, getting a consensus would be difficult. Also, the ultimate decision for or against may be tied to the contexts that have the money and skills to lobby politicians.

Social policy and personal context come together in the issue of the recent attention to the alleged "breast cancer gene" (Cowley, 1993). Publicity surrounding the idea that breast cancer is inherited is co-emerging with women having preventative mastectomies when they have a family history of breast cancer but no evidence of cancer themselves. Here parallogic becomes important in considering that what is produced in the context of medical research and publicized in the context of the media may have important effects when it enters into the contexts of women who are less likely to have the education and skills necessary to fully understand what the concept of a breast cancer gene means. What is exploratory and merely suggestive at the research context may be seen as prescriptive in the personal context. A parallogical view involves seeing as the person with a family history might see, and in so doing, making researchers, physicians, and medical policy makers think carefully about legitimizing preventative mastectomy or publicizing the concept of a breast cancer gene without a full understanding of its implications.

As I will develop in greater detail in the next section on "realities," parallogical thinking is a jumping board to thinking in terms of "a way" as opposed to the more conventional focus on "the way." Realities and parallogic both suggest thinking about multiplex contexts of meaning contents that make it possible to seat judgment in contexts without resorting to universals.

Parallogic is created in an intersection between thinking about human subjectivity and nonsummativity. Subjectivity provides the notion of specific relevant social construction, interpretation, and reflexiveness, while nonsummativity allows us to place such creations in the flexible reference point of context. In so doing, thinking about human subjective meaning can be explored beyond the trap laid by linear causality, which manifests as level.

This presents a new brand of theory to be added to the modeling of the relationship between the individual mind and the social self. In my journal article version of the parallogic argument, I express this potential in the title, "Parallogic: As Mind Meets Context" (Hanson, 1989b). By seating reasoning within context, I go beyond the universal of reason. This adds to thinking about the relationship between mental and social processes, in that it challenges the notion that a lack of reason is evidence of a breakdown in the ability to reason. It offers that it may be fruitful to separate universal reason from contextual reasoning by eliminating all possible errors made by judging without native awareness of context.

Research can be challenged to examine those assumptions and derivative procedures that are based on universal nomothetic principles. A multiplex view of *ways* rather than *way* upsets a great deal of effort in terms of using average tendencies to conclude about universal properties. Instead contexts, in what may be conventionally thought of as outlier analysis, become the focal unit.

Everyday experience can draw upon parallogic by prompting people to think carefully about judgments of others that may be based on relative difference rather than attributed deviance, inferiority, or abnormality. If you were in his or her place, would you do the same thing? Would you give up, too, if you were constantly told you were inferior, sick, too short, too fat, ugly?

REALITIES

Realties is a means of seeing experience as situated in multiverse, a way, rather than the conventional focus on universe, the way.

By allowing that meaning is context-specific and therefore inherently true, it is possible to offer an alternative to the idea that reality is singular and universal. Seeing the importance of subjective human group interpretations in contexts and how these constructions enter into behavior means seeing worlds of mean-ing rather than a single world—*a way* rather than *the way*.

It is possible in this manner to set aside notions of sanity, insanity, normal-ity, abnormality, truth, and fact as universals in favor of viewing what is taken as sane or normal in context. This does not necessarily contradict a view of objective universal reality so much as it provides an alternative epistemology. A realities view does not negate a reality view, but a reality view does negate a realities view.

The power of a notion of multiplex realities lies in delving into the relation-ship between theory, observation, and epistemology. Specifically it makes it possible to examine the permeation of positivist thinking into theory. Discus-sion of universal law on the theoretical level often comes into play when ques-tions of methodology are raised, but less so in the explicit question of how a positivist mind-set colors theoretical thinking in general.

I argue that while the issue of human subjectivity now has a long and noble history, it has never been carried through to consider what it means for the basic issues of epistemology and derivative notions of science that I treat here. While subjectivity as a human characteristic has a broad base of support, the implications of this trait for a model of human behavior in terms of the philo-sophical basis of epistemology is absent. Because of this the potential of a wholes approach as a springboard to a notion of realities has been missed.

Previous approaches have fallen into two notable dead ends: the micro/ macro debate in the case of symbolic interaction, and antipositivism in the case of postmodernism. I will not belabor here how a wholes approach can transcend the micro/macro debate, as this is covered extensively in previous sections of this book. I add the argument here that the antipositivist critiques that have occurred have remained trapped by the dictates of positivism in that they argue against singular reality, but do not actually challenge positivism by providing an alternative. "There is one reality." No, there isn't. I ask, what is there? I offer multiverse and realities.

This is a deceptively simple step. It goes beyond the question of whether or not there is a single reality by allowing for multiplex realities as situated in contexts. In so doing it is possible to avoid the nihilism of antipositivism while working in an explicit epistemology for the idea of human subjectivity. This makes it possible to begin thinking in terms of context-specific reference points rather than universals in the process of analysis and intervention. At this juncture the demarcation of context and content becomes useful. It is possible to think about what is meaningful in context in terms of why one and not another individual case exhibits a behavior under like conditions of content.

The question of pathology in intimate relations is an apt example of the importance of realities epistemology. A universal bias in questions like mental illness, spousal abuse, anorexia, obesity, or incest may add to the problems associated with these categories for the individuals involved. Focusing on the pathological or deviant nature of some targeted behavior relative to some alleged universal standard for behavior may add to the guilt, pain, and low self-esteem likely to be associated with any of these conditions. Furthermore, by focusing on the condition in one individual, behavior may be magnified or problems may change into other manifestations. The importance of a realities view here is seen particularly in mental illness, as the alleged universal of mental health has proven elusive to empirical discovery, while mental illness proliferates. Notable works here are Srole et al.'s discovery that in excess of one half of a randomly selected sample of people showed significant mental illness symptoms (1978) and Rosenhan's chronicle of how an array of research confederates were labeled and sustained with a definition of mental illness in the process of being admitted into a mental hospital, even though they had no previous problems (1976).

Realities adds to this by discarding the notion that there is such a thing as mental health or illness in the universal sense. Instead the focus becomes why one person instead of another is taken as sick under like conditions. An implicit criticism of the clinical realm underpins the Rosenhan and Srole studies: clinicians do not know what mental illness is. I argue that this indictment is a projection, not of clinical incompetence, but rather the content of cultures that promote belief in mental health as an opposite of mental illness. Several questions co-emerge from realities epistemology. Why do we have these clinicians? Are they there to foster the belief in mental health via the definition and management of mental illness? If mental illness is not the issue, what is? Experiments like Rosenhan's show up the nature of mental illness patienting when an artificial move to create a patient is made. The missing question here is, if Rosenhan can have "normal" people turned into mental illness patients, can anyone do it? How did the rest of the patients get there?

It is possible to use the notion of realities to argue that the process of considering someone sick is rooted in intimate contexts and their unique brands of meaning; the cultural content of a clinical intervention is secondary to the desire to create a patient. All Rosenhan did was coach research confederates on how to respond to questions from clinicians; the rest of the process took on a momentum all its own. What was absent from his experiment was the influence an intimate context may have on the process of patienting, which may be a life-long, even generational, creation in intimate contexts. Further, a model of the clinical realm as defining and maintaining patients presumes that clinicians control the process. I argue that the degree to which clinicians have control is at least minimal, and possibly nonexistent, in that they have no participation in the initial move to seek treatment or in treatment-shopping among clinicians.

Realities has been grasped wholeheartedly, although I sense the term has never arisen, in the realm of product marketing. Here the problems of universalism have been widely acknowledged. Different age groups, cultures, regions, genders, and so on have vastly differing meaning sets leading to what they will buy. It would be futile to try selling life insurance and burial plots to 18-year-olds, because, as I once read, "At that age, death is just an ugly rumor." The target market becomes key. The relevance of this line of thinking has become more obvious currently as the largest single market is the baby boom, or "Big Chill," generation. The crowd that was targeted for Lee Iacocca's original Mustang car in the 1960s was also the target for the "mini vans" in the 1980s. The influence on marketing that the particular reality of people born in the post-World War II baby boom has is reflected in the predominance of "soft rock" radio stations, often with preselected sets of music. No less relevant to the realities argument has been the simultaneous, less numerous but equally context-focused stations focusing on the "big band era" and "hard rock." In each case the message is the same, universalism has a limited scope. A fully spending market is one conceived of as multiverses.

Problems in presumptions of universe correlated with the development of legislation to promote equal opportunity in employment practices. Data from many sources showed that while hiring and promotion practices were stated to be fair, they discriminated against women. Assuming a model of the ideal employee that was male-centered disadvantaged women because they were judged less ideal by definition. This translated into a situation in Ontario where women earned approximately 60 cents to men's one dollar, and women were grossly underrepresented in high status jobs. Concepts like "chilly climate," "glass ceiling," and "sloped playing field" were used to make policy writers aware that the universe was different for women than men in ways that meant that equally qualified women were disadvantaged. Employment equity legislation was designed to overcome some of these disadvantages by judging men and women on an equal basis relevant to employment skills and experience.

The heritage of a realities view is tied to models of human subjectivity as linked to models of epistemology. The notion of subjectivity, extended to the question of what and how we can know, suggests a multiverse view of realities. Carried through, this means directing attention to a context specific, rather than universal, analysis. In essence this means going after *a way* as opposed to *the way* of explaining phenomena.

The theoretical advance comes in carrying through the idea of human subjectivity into epistemology. Previously subjectivity has been accepted, but remained trapped by moves to universalism, either implicitly or explicitly. As often as not, this comes from trying to move from the theoretical to the methodological, where methods remain dominated by positivist thinking. It is simultaneously possible to escape the "is so, is not, is so, is not" debate that has typified antipositivist critiques. To reiterate, I offer that to argue against something is to maintain that thing. To transcend the argument means doing something different. To this end, realities as a conception of multiverse transcends universe.

Methods need to be rethought to allow for an alternative approach to analysis. Outlier analysis hints at the principle of context-specific analysis. Analysis of variance as a cornerstone of inferential statistics could be rethought as a *complex* of models as opposed to *the* model, which explains the most, though almost never the majority of variance. Average tendency and aggregation need to be rethought completely, because they require assumptions of universe.

In as much as realities suggests rethinking universalism in the abstract, it challenges acceptance of single interpretations that may not reflect the context of a given group. The permeation of universalism into everyday consciousness is detectable in the phrase, "They say . . ." This alleged *they* as a product of universal knowledge wanders into common language. The importance and concurrent danger in making life choices based on the alleged universal can be seen in the seesaw nature of medical wisdom, each presented as true, and as a universal in its own right. "Experts have shown" that breast-feeding, sugar, oat bran, cholesterol, red wine, red meat, alcohol, and so on, have good, bad, or no effects on health at various points in time. The wholehearted reversal of medical wisdom on a variety of issues is commonplace, unless one limits the time frame to a single incident.

To discuss this, I asked a class consisting mostly of nurses who had been working in the profession of medicine for many (some as long as 30 years) to come up with a single treatment or recommendation that had not been reversed in the course of their careers. They found none, but an abundance of examples where obverse treatments had occurred, sometimes going back and forth several times. Universalism in medicine relies on the notion that because reality is singular, what is found in any objectively conducted and controlled study indicates a universal law of human health, even, often especially, where these studies are conducted on animals. Perhaps the flip-flop nature of health wisdom reflects the need to abandon an "acontextual" view of objective reality in favor of a contextual view of subjective realities.

Chapter 6

Communication

Communication refers to the exchange of information.

In this chapter I deal with issues and concepts surrounding communication, which I define as the exchange of information. My ideas draw heavily on the work of Watzlawick, Bavelas, and Jackson's *Pragmatics of Human Communication* (1967), which remains a cornerstone in thinking about human communication. I picked up this conception for my own empirical work and have extended it on the theoretical front by adding that it is possible to improve the model by removing the pathology question (Hanson, 1989a, 1991c) and substantively by seating the center of derivative communication patterns in emotion rather than cognition.

I take the definition of communication as information exchange in the broadest possible sense in order to allow for a broad range of kinds of information exchange in various systems. My focus in the later sections of this chapter will be on communication in human groups. The principles may apply to other types of systems. In fact many of the principles that underlie the model of human communication I present began with the observation of animal communication.

This is in itself an interesting question to consider from a wholes approach. Does human communication differ, and if so how, from that of other species or physical phenomena? It was thought for a long time that humans differed from other species in terms of their ability to have language. Recently other animals, such as dolphins, have been found to have language of their own in terms of sound emissions.

The wholes approach I take extends the question of human versus other by capturing modes of communication that do not rely solely on sound emission. I learned from Norman W. Bell that this was originally suggested by Gregory Bateson after watching movies of otters. On close examination he noticed that the actions of play fighting and fighting to kill or injure were essentially similar. This raised the question of how the otters know when they are fighting to play versus fighting to kill. This spawned the theory of metacommunication to capture the idea that there is information exchanged that lets participants know how to interpret information. If the ostensible information is the same, batting your mate across the face with a paw, interpreting this act as aggression or play requires additional information.

This spawns a two part, or dual, model of communication to capture both the direct observable forms of communication and the indirect forms of information exchange that are tied to the relationship rather than derivative parts. An act of communication like swatting a mate is understood only in terms of the relationship between the mates and the context of the group. Any form of direct observable communication like words, squeaks, or body movements needs to be interpreted both in the context of the relationship and in the content of the wider group. A gesture of a sexually explicit insult may have a different meaning in a different culture. The meaning of this gesture will vary again within a relationship context. It may be a term of endearment, or insult, or seduction. The point here is that the gesture or word itself must be interpreted within the frame of the relationship before it can be understood, or the content must be decoded relative to its native context.

Here the tool of parallogic is useful to consider examples of this principle. In looking at videotapes of 45 families with aged members, some of whom were identified as senile dementia patients, I was constantly reminded of the need to use the nature of the relationship to decode and interpret what given actions and words meant to the family members. I recall one couple where the man used a constant stream of compliments, endearments, and stroking gestures. I was confused when this form of communication appeared to upset the woman, causing her to shake, withdraw, and ask to stop the videotaping. After viewing the tape several times I began to see that the ostensible content of his communication, gestures and words, though culturally interpretable as loving, worked in this relationship to control the woman and to keep her from offering any opinions or having her wishes acted out.

Another couple confirmed the principle of a dual model of communication in precisely the opposite direction. This couple constantly insulted each other. I was in a quandary as to why this constant derogation did not appear to upset them. Upon more extensive examination, it became clear that this was a way of diffusing conflict and was a form of play for the couple that seemed to allow both to participate. In both cases focus on the content or direct modes of communication was insufficient to understand what communication meant in context.

Throughout transitions of life there is a learning process in terms of communication on the levels of content and context. Take the example of trying to adjust to a new job. Even if trained as an academic, going to a new university will likely mean that new language and gesture contents will have to be learned, along with how and when to use them and what they mean relative to the dynamics of a context. My own recent experience with this transition is apt. To adjust, I had to learn a whole new array of short forms for courses. What was listed in the calendar as number 3300 was referred to in the common language of the department as 330. Students have likely experienced similar confusion when they switch institutions or start new courses and learn new institutional "lingo" and the particular modes to interpret this information in the relational context of different courses with different teachers.

In policy it is possible to consider the relationship between what is said or stated and what is meant, and how this suggests acting. When a government official says that the recession is over, what does this mean? Does it mean the recession is over or that the recession is continuing but the government needs to foster the belief that it is over to get people spending or incumbents re-elected? The content "recession is over" can be contextualized on several dimensions. One of the most telling here is sequence. It is possible to interpret the content in the context of events that precede it, like an election being called, recent figures that unemployment is up, last year's similar statement, and so on. A famous example here is Richard Nixon's televised statement "I am not a crook" in the initial stages of what became the Watergate scandal. The point from a dual model of communication is to look for the total message being communicated. Does making a statement that one is doing nothing mean that the person is afraid of being caught at something? Or, does the need to make a statement itself, rather than say nothing, mean that the statement can be interpreted contextually as its obverse? An interesting example here, suggested by the helpful development editor of this book, is the requirement that U.S. Senators and Representatives be polite to one another. They get around this by saying the exact opposite of what they mean, for example, "I am sure the Senator from California is *not* a (insert the desired insult here)."

My ideas about communication as analytically dual phenomena are extensions of the principles of communication outlined by Watzlawick et al. (1967) as tied to my conceptions of the content–context separation and parallogic. Taking up the concepts of previous work provides a means of integrating groundbreaking insights of the past with more recent developments in theory and empirical investigation that have led me to elaborate a wholes approach. It allows consideration of issues like gender and race relations, which have proliferated since 1967, as well as basics of a sociological approach like structure and class, which were not integrated into the original theory.

The relevance of including a chapter on communication in my presentation of a wholes approach lies in sharing these important insights in a less abstract form than the original text and in integrating communication theory into a general systems theory approach as updated by recent work. For research, the message is to target communication in its full range rather than concentrate solely on surface projections like language and gestures. This makes any method that relies on verbal communication, either written or spoken, difficult to interpret within the terms of reference of a dual model of communication. Everyday relevance lies in using a model of communication that focuses not on just what is said, but on what is meant as well, to help in planning actions. Is now a good time to buy a house based on what the president or prime minister has just said about an economic recovery beginning?

REPORT AND COMMAND

Report is pure information.
Command is how to interpret this information.

The last section spelled out in general terms the principle of a dual model of communication that corresponds with my content–context separation. This section draws the separation more specifically into the demarcation of report and command as developed by Watzlawick et al. (1967). The difference between the two is that content and context provide greater focus on the broader social context in which interpersonal communication takes place, while report and command home in on interpersonal communication. Thus the two overlap.

Report refers to the pure kernel of information in communication, verbal in the case of humans. Command is information about the report that helps people interpret the meaning of the report: gestures, voice tone, and sequence. To give an example, the report "I love you," if said in a gentle tone with wide eyes, means one thing. Said through gritted teeth it means another. If said in the sequence "Of course, I love you," it means something else again. In each case the report is qualified by information about the relationship that is conveyed in the commands of gestures, voice tone, and sequence. It is not possible to understand what the report means in the context without looking at the command as well.

This separation becomes crucial on two fronts. Attention to report and command spawned the theory that disjunctures between these two aspects of communication could be at the heart of mental illness. Persons who are part of a context where messages are mixed between report and command may have trouble coping in other contexts. For instance a child who is told, "I love you, and only do what is best for you," before getting beaten may carry this association between love and violence into other relational contexts where it is inappropriate, say with schoolmates. It could later lead to seeking relationships with persons who have also grown up with love–violence links in communication. The theory in terms of schizophrenia came to be seen as a double bind, which I will elaborate in detail in the next section. Here the central point is to understand the separation of report and command and what it can mean for the process of communication in general without necessarily focusing on pathology.

In intimate relations the expression "you're not hearing each other" has wandered into pop psychology. Report and command would point out that problems in understanding intimates may be traced to an inability to read commands, or messages about the relationship, such that no amount of verbal communication helps. Unfortunately, interventions into these problems tend to focus on report communication and work on expression and eliminating conflict, either through a cognitive model of behavior or an exchange model. My own work points out that these projections into communication are merely surface manifestations that are secondary to emotional patterns (Hanson, 1989a). Therefore working at the surface level of communication is unlikely to uproot the emotional distress that appears as difficulty communicating.

I recall the expression "The best contracts are between enemies." This suggests an organizational application of report and command. The expression refers to the idea that a contract of words on paper is most likely to be successful when those entering into the contract distrust or even hate each other because the emotional loading forces an agreement that takes nothing for granted, so every conceivable detail is written down. By contrast, when entering into a spousal situation or business with a friend or family member, it is likely that the people will have a very loose arrangement with little or nothing written down. In contrast to the enemies who began with a very pat formal contract, those who began with mutual fondness may end up as enemies. Consider the problems in the succession of control of a business when it is passing from parent to child; problems in dividing the children, pets, and property of a spousal situation; or sharing the family cottage when children become adults. Here it is possible to think about how the report (written) versus command (relational) comes into play in financial or legal agreements.

I can think of no more apt demonstration of the report and command separation in policy than Hitler's promise to not continue expanding Germany via invasion. This is a situation where acting based on report (verbal promises) without considering command (the relationship) led, in equifinal fashion, to war. It is possible to consider whether or not acting on report even hastened the process by encouraging invasion. The point is to consider not just what is said and contracted, but what it meant in terms of the relationship in question.

My presentation is derived directly from Watzlawick et al.'s (1967) conception. In the original the authors seem to draw on several areas in their formulation, including mathematics, psychology, evolution, and anthropology. When they speak of content they are talking about the digital forms of information in communication. This refers to arbitrary associations between meaning and word. It captures the dimension that with digital communication there is no inherently meaningful association between a word and its symbol, the word. It has been agreed at some point that the two will be linked. Another way of putting it is that "[t]here is no particular reason why the three letters 'c-a-t' should denote a particular animal. . ." (Watzlawick et al., 1967, pp. 61–62). Or there is nothing particularly "twolike" about a "2." My conception is consistent with this notion and extends it to sociological issues like race, class, and gender, which go into types of word–thing associations. Context in my model is consistent with their reference to "relationship." (Watzlawick et al., 1967, p. 51). It is consistent with both models to see the context of communication as the qualifier of content.

For theories of social behavior, the importance of report and command lies in beginning the process of explaining why one and not another person or case act in a particular way under like structural conditions. Explanation based on aggregate patterns of cases that share some structural trait or traits, though providing a means of estimation in populations, breaks down at the case level. This harks back to the issue of variance unexplained. Even though aggregate analysis of commonality may net out a model of average tendency, when you go to look at an individual case, the odds are against that single model explaining it. Explained variance in the social sciences rarely exceeds 40%. By separating report and command, content and context, it is possible to begin theorizing the individual case. Why has poverty and discrimination led to violence here, but not next door? This provides a means of overriding the most glaring critique of structural explanations, which may explain why someone commits a crime, but falls down completely when stretched to explain why someone else, under the same structural conditions, does not.

Research strategies must incorporate the relational into all aspects of design, collection, and analysis. Minimally this means retaining relational units in order that relationships in fact exist in the data set. In analysis it means developing techniques for interpreting, or "decoding," verbal reports in terms of the command context. Written transcripts are useless without knowledge of the context. The same goes for any data derived from individuals or verbal information alone.

Report and command provide a useful, albeit thorny, wedge into understanding our own relationships. It is useful in the sense that it is possible to think about not just one's words but how they are taken in context. It is thorny in the sense that it is not likely that context is knowable for the individual. If the whole is greater than the sum of its parts, and this whole is context, no part has access to context. This may suggest drawing on others to help understand one's own relationships, or looking at data like videos and pictures. It might be useful to look at the family album, particularly back in time, to gain insight into oneself and one's self in relationships.

YOU CANNOT NOT COMMUNICATE

There is no such thing as no communication.

You cannot not communicate. This is one of the basic axioms of communication as spelled out by Watlawick et al. (1967, pp. 48–51). What it means is that because everything is related to everything and causality is cybernetic, all forms of behavior are communication. There is no such thing as noncommunication in that not responding may tell as much as responding. This is particularly relevant in face to face communication in that, while no verbal or report communication takes place, body and facial gestures (commands) will provide information.

One of my favorite examples of the principle that you cannot not communicate is a scene from the 1977 movie *Annie Hall* where Diane Keaton and Woody Allen are having their first private conversation as a prelude to dating. They are carrying on a verbal conversation and at the same time the audience is told what the characters are thinking and responding to what is said and not said in subtitles as follows.

> Keaton: I dabble? Listen to me—what a jerk.
> Allen: You are a great-looking girl.
> Keaton: He probably thinks I'm a yo-yo.
> Allen: I wonder what she looks like naked.
> Keaton: I'm not smart enough for him. Hang in there.

There is a constant flow of information back and forth that may operate completely separate from verbal communication or even in direct opposition to what is being said.

Even in trying to not say or do anything, one person's communication can be inferred and created by others. I observed this repeatedly in my observations of families with aged members. Whole sets of feelings and opinions were constructed for persons in the process of defining them as sick. "Dad is worried about money." "Mother, you can't feel that way." "Honey, you don't want steak for dinner."

What this sets up is a model of communication that is a full set or context. Because there is no such thing as noncommunication, analysis of communication must be done in terms of relational, co-emergent units. As much as in the previous discussion of report and command, this makes it crucial to focus on dyadic units as the minimum and look at back and forth sequences before being able to understand what is going on in context. No individual report is relevant without seeing how others react to it. Furthermore, it is necessary to look for patterns of constructed meaning sets that prompt behavior but are formed at a level outside the visible manifestations of individual communication. Constructions like: "Susan can have no privacy." "David is not very bright." "We can't interrupt Lisa's nap to get the cookbook, but it's OK if we're after Dad's pipe." These concepts may never appear verbally or in active communication, but are nonetheless important communications. They may contribute to Susan's difficulty with intimacy, David's failing at school despite a genius-level IQ, or Lisa's feeling of low self-worth.

Such constructs, because they emerge at the relational rather than the individual level, are likely to be unrecognized by the participants. This becomes particularly confounding to individuals when active or verbal communication confounds the constructs of noncommunication. A person is being told one thing, yet the whole context acts in contradiction to this formal message. "This is for your own good, you're too young," is said when parents cancel an adolescent girl's first mixed party. Her insecurities and embarrassment in dealing with boys her age is heightened when they add, "Why don't you lose some weight first." So she feels unattractive and the offered reason is her weight. This spawns secret eating, accompanied by public dieting and exercising enforced by parents. The stated problem is her weight, yet no matter how thin she gets the communicated message is that she is never lovable. In sum, the central point of the idea that you cannot not communicate is that communication, because it is dual and relational, must be looked at as a whole set of behaviors and ostensible nonbehaviors before it can be understood.

In intimacy this principle shows up in forms of behavior like the bifurcating phenomena of bulimia and anorexia. One can imagine the example above of the adolescent girl who lives in a relational context where all her problems are attributed to her being overweight. She enters into an inescapable pattern whereby eating is the central definition of her life. When depressed she binge eats. This depresses her more so she diets, binges, purges, or takes laxatives. Even losing weight does not change the fact that there appears to be no means of feeling loved and of having self-esteem. When she is thin her problem is loose morals or lack of intelligence. When she is fat her problem is fat. There are thus no conditions for being loved. She carries this into relationships outside the family and even though she controls her weight, she has difficulty with intimate relationships and seeks partners who reinforce this conditional love and low self-esteem. The message of conditional love and self-disgust has been communicated very effectively to this woman even though it was never stated.

The novel *Red Storm Rising* by Tom Clancy (1986) chronicles a fictional war between the Soviet Union and the NATO forces. As each side tries to infer the plans of the other, be it where the submarines are or when they plan to invade, there is careful attention to the principle *you cannot not communicate.* The process of figuring out a plan is closely tied to what the enemy is not doing. They haven't attacked here so this means they will likely attack there. Why didn't they attack at dawn? The point here is that in a linked system, noncommunication, as we may think about it conventionally, is as important as ostensible communication. An organizational parallel, recalling my earlier discussion, is the way IBM did nothing in the microcomputer market for many years after Apple opened up the field and brands proliferated. Reading this, one can infer a long-term plan to watch competition as indicative of the market for microcomputers and let smaller competitors kill each other off. Possible short-term gains were forfeited in the plan to make much greater long-term profits.

What is the message communicated when a government decides to have no policy on abortion? Pro-choice advocates might interpret this nonaction as a communication that abortion is a health service that requires no special legislation. For them, this would be a favorable step. Pro-life advocates might take the contrary view that this in effect legalizes murder and, as such, is a major setback. Here the contextual importance of interpreting any form of communication is exemplified. The context here is set up between each side of the debate and the government and the three participants in total. This can lead to a number of significant events such as bombing abortion clinics, attacks on physicians who perform abortions, or blocking clinic entrances to force confrontation with women who are trying to have an abortion.

The notion that you cannot not communicate has had a tremendous impact on theories of interpersonal relations and mental illness. It made it possible to go looking for "invisible," in the sense of not ostensible or conscious, constructions that may be at the center of a targeted behavior. Counseling couples, divorce mediation, labor negotiation, and other related activities all rely on this principle. Often, the now popular practice of "facilitating" works at getting hidden noncommunicated agendas and ideas to the surface of ostensible communication in order to bring about resolution of conflict or spur creative thinking.

Doing research guided by this idea means collecting and analyzing data that allows spotting the relationship between communication and noncommunication. Initially this means retaining dyads as the minimum unit. Then, continuous time segments and sequences of communication must be observed. In this manner it is possible to see how not doing things fits with doing things in order to sort out the contextual meanings of communication. Actions and inactions must be attributed with equal status. Silence becomes as relevant as talk and must therefore be built into data collection and analysis in a way that recognizes this.

There is value in the principle *you cannot not communicate* to issues of self-esteem, confidence, and empowerment. We can never escape or avoid communication. Everything we do or do not do communicates something. Where there are threats to one's self-esteem or confidence, feelings of worthlessness may prompt a person to try to withdraw. Recognizing that this withdrawal itself accepts and reinforces the degradation suggests the idea that one might as well take the risk of direct action because there is nothing to lose and much to gain.

DOUBLE BIND

A double bind is a situation that is inherently contradictory,
intense, and inescapable.

"Speak only when you're spoken to!" the Queen sharply interrupted her.

"But if everybody obeyed that rule," said Alice, who was always ready for a little argument, "and if you only spoke when you were spoken to, and the other person always waited for you to begin, you see nobody would ever say anything, so that—"

"Ridiculous!" cried the Queen. "Why don't you see child—"

(Carroll, 1865/1981, p. 200)

The double bind concept draws on the notion of report and command and articulates a theory about the basis of mental illness in family contexts. It models relational situations that are prone to driving people crazy, like the situation between Alice and the Red Queen. It was first developed by Bateson, Jackson, Haley, and Weakland (1956/1976) and has three essential elements that relate to a dual model of communication.

First, there are two or more persons involved in an intense relationship. This forms the basis for defining the phenomena and further defines it in terms of significance, in that it is not likely observed in casual or short-term relationships.

Second, something is said and something is asserted about the original something. The original statement and the assertion about it are contradictory such that there is no way to respond to one without violating the other. It is like the situation when a parent gives a son two neckties. When he puts one on the parent says, "So you didn't like the other one."

Third, there is no escape from the situation. This lies on two fronts, the intensity of the relationship means that it cannot be avoided, even through physical separation, and there is no such thing as noncommunicating, so a wrong response must occur no matter what.

Over time people who live and learn in such situations develop means of relating to others that are grounded in this type of painful, frustrating, and irresolvable relationship. It can be analogized to Alice stepping through the looking glass into a world of vast contradiction. In intimate relationships the paradoxes between elements of communication are often found in disjunctures between report and command. "How can you say I don't love you? I'm your mother, aren't I?" "You've been just like a mother to me." "You look so pretty, no one will notice how much weight you have gained." "What a great dress, your hips don't even look big." Nonverbal gestures like facial expression and voice tone would also enter into this but are difficult to approximate on paper.

There is a relational pattern set up such that people may have trouble knowing what is real or appropriate at any given time since there is no such thing as correctness in context. Because the situation is rooted in perpetual paradox, whatever is said, or not said, is wrong.

In intimate relations the concept of a double bind can be illustrated in family contexts and mental illness. One of the most famous examples of issues of metacommunication and irresolvable paradoxes is Laing and Esterson's *Sanity, Madness and the Family* (1964). Here a number of families with identified schizophrenic patients are presented. In each case it is possible to see situations where there are irresolvable paradoxes, such as growing independence concurrent with restriction of independence. Acts of oppression are accompanied by verbal declarations of love. Unlike Alice these patients cannot step out of the relationship.

Imagine the situation of a new employee, a woman who was told that she was hired, in competition with many others, based on demonstrated excellence, and that she will now be expected to contribute to the organization in order to gain favor and advance. As soon as she starts working, she notices that the immediate superiors in the hierarchy are threatened and become hostile, and degrade her performance the more she succeeds. In order to advance within the organization or move to another, she needs to maintain the accomplishments that got her the job in the first place. However, the harder she works and the more she achieves, the greater the tendency of those over her, less skilled and accomplished, to be threatened and therefore try to deny or downplay her accomplishments. This situation is inescapable in that in order to leave she must achieve, but the current organization works strongly against this at every turn, directly by increasing her workload relative to others, and indirectly by convincing her that she is not as good as others or is in fact failing by achieving.

When her performance has five scores at the very top of the scale "excellent," the department head points out that she has a problem with the sixth because it was only "very good." When she is chosen from among all the new employees to sit on the most important upper-level committee in the organization, the chair begins to complain that she needs to spend more time in her office when he is around.

I sense there is a parallel between the concept of a double bind and the concept of the arms race if we extend the premises. If we consider parts as being nations rather than individuals, it is possible to see two countries such as the U.S. and the Soviet Union since World War II as the intensely related members of a relationship. The term defense itself holds the elements of a paradox in that the process of defense is getting ready to attack. Recent history may, however, provide a twist on the issue of inescapability. The long-term perceived inescapability of the situation, if we stop spending on war they will attack, fueled the process for decades. However, the U.S. managed to outspend and outlast the Soviet Union, which has since become divided. The Soviet Union stopped playing by default. The double bind lesson here is interesting. Perhaps military defense spending is escapable.

A situation perceived as perpetually double binding was in fact resolvable if one of the players stopped playing its part. One way to critique my analogy is to say that it was therefore not a double bind at all. I argue that it was because it was perceived as such and a parallogical shift into a different system of logic broke the paradox as far as the Soviet Union was concerned. However, the U.S. appears to still be double bound in that their continued war posture has led to inescapability as new counter threateners co-emerge.

In my own work I have been extending the notion of the double bind by removing the sanity question from analysis of mental illness. A realities view allows separating the principles of paradox in communication from issues of whether or not such paradoxes are crazy. I got onto this separation when I observed that superficial communication paradoxes did not seem to explain the process of trying to define someone as a mental illness patient (Hanson, 1991c). This became particularly relevant when I noted severe paradox in families identified as nonpathological. This led me to model communication as a relevant property of human communication groups, but one determined by emotional properties.

Double bind was a key element of the theories and practices of intimate relations that were revolutionized by general systems theory approaches in the 1950s and 1960s. Family therapy was established as a legitimate area of study and mode of intervention into mental illness. The journal *Family Process* was started. Unfortunately research has not kept pace with theoretical developments. It seems to have fallen into the cracks between clinical and research and scholarly pursuits. The majority of work done in this tradition is focused on clinical agendas and observations and applied disciplines, rather than research and theory development. This needs to be done before the theoretical core of concepts erodes completely as they are compromised for purposes of expediency. Double bind provides a means of seeing irresolvable paradoxes that may be leading to intense stress. Recall the case of the junior woman employee above. Perhaps seeing the paradoxical nature of a relationship such as this can help individuals understand that there is no personal blame. You cannot be good enough to fix this because it is set up as not fixable by definition. Perhaps seeing the impasse will allow an individual to maintain self-esteem and reduce stress by escaping a double bind.

Chapter 7

Emotion

Feeling.

Emotion. The first frontier? I argue that the pursuit of knowledge about human behavior has often been a denial of human characteristics, notably emotion. Supplanting feeling with thinking in models of human phenomena may have been an approach that has kept analysis from getting at the essence of human behavior. In this sense, emotion can be seen as the first frontier for inquiry, one that has been denied or paved over but has yet to be explored.

Conventional investigations and the models that guide them have assumed a linear, logical epistemology for human behavior both in terms of the role of the analyst and the targeted phenomena. It is possible that this overlay of linearity and logic is based more on ideological or political motivation to believe in logic or to control human behavior within a particular mind-set than on the degree to which it can explain human behavior. The key question here is how much, or how little, of human behavior can be explained based on a model of rationality?

I argue that the purview of logic is very limited, and unless inquiry escapes these limits, pressing problems like racism, sexism, global degradation, and armed conflict will remain perpetually inexplicable. Did the Gulf War make sense? Was the verdict in the original Rodney King trial in Los Angeles, or the rioting that followed it, logical? What is a reasonable explanation of sexual assault? Is it rational to destroy the rainforests? The epistemology of logic means that explanations within this frame are limited to the cognitive, the rational, the sensible. The tendency for logic to fail as an explanation is as great as the degree to which emotion is central to human behavior.

Over time, dissatisfaction with rationality as an explanation for human behavior has led not to discarding the model, but rather to the creation of a dumping ground for phenomena that are not explained. This has come in two forms: disease and nonrationality. With disease, the move is to attribute any inexplicable behavior, like spousal violence, inappropriate shouting, or showing anger, to some aberrant disorder of the body and relegate the phenomena to a pathological category and apply a medical model. Nonrationality, or irrationality, surfaces as a way to classify behavior as outside the purview of explanation within a model of rationality. In both cases, however, emotional behavior is functionally equivalent to inexplicable behavior.

This can be as easily attributed to the failure of a model of logic itself to capture the full range of human behavior, as to some pathological origin to inexplicable behavior. In this sense saying that something is pathological is not an acceptable response to the fact that it is inexplicable. It is possible to argue that it is the model that needs to be improved rather than the people who need to be cured or controlled.

By using a model of rationality to try to capture human behavior, emotion has effectively been modeled based on what it is not rather than what it is. Rendering any emotional response as outside the purview of the model effectively means that it cannot be explained. There is an interesting parallel in considerations of gender. Simone de Beauvoir (1949/1989) pointed out the idea of sexual relativity in *The Second Sex*. Woman was modeled relative to man and as such found inexplicable, necessitating models of pathology, without considering the possibility of a "woman-centric" model of women.

Emotion has been modeled relative to logic via the same principle and has also been found inexplicable. Here the argument is metatheoretical on two grounds. First, there are similarities in terms of the structural attributes of models of gender and emotion. Second, and perhaps more importantly, the rendering of logic may be tied to the substantive association of emotion with women. It is possible to argue that the relegation of emotion to relative or second status has co-emerged in social historical context with the ideology of sexism.

In light of this, a move to undo the suppression of emotion from models of human behavior may simultaneously provide more gender-balanced theories. Providing an alternative to the assumed monolith of objectivity and rationality may offer a means of humanizing models of humans by recouping a salient, and as I will argue in the next section, higher order, characteristic. In this manner the conceptual jackets designed to fit humans will be better tailored by allowing for curves and movement.

The difference between a model of emotion and a model of emotion as irrationality can be illustrated by considering a case of spousal abuse. One evening a spouse comes home to find his or her spouse cooking meatloaf for dinner. The noncooking spouse goes wild and beats the cooking spouse unconscious and then begins crying and apologizing. A model of irrationality would look for some pathological origin to this. Was the beating spouse drunk, schizophrenic, having a seizure? A model of emotion would look long range at the patterned cycles of emotional reactions between the spouses that, though not rational, were redundant, hence amenable to analysis. Here it may emerge that feelings of self-disgust in both spouses, fueled by recent loss of employment co-emergent with weight gain, led to escalating tension and pain between the couple. Meatloaf became the spark that ignited this residual pain and self-debasement, leading to dissipation. The key difference between the models lies in how the phenomena are unitized. The model of suprarationality allows for emergent contextual emotion, while a model of irrationality necessitates breaking up the couple into individuals in order to feed them into models of disease.

"I know it doesn't make sense, but they sold millions of those dolls." "The housing market would turn around instantly if people stopped being afraid that they are going to lose their jobs." The message of a model of emotion here is that human group emotions are not something that are amenable to analysis or intervention based on rationality. Breaking down some desired consumer spending into its components—"let's make them gender neutral," "how about offering a free lawn mower," "begin the ads with 'The recession is over'" will not get at the heart of what attracts and deters humans from purchases. Individual events such as a purchase are fueled and conversely dampened by how any given stimuli, like changes in advertising or product, are reacted to by context-level emotions.

In terms of social policy a cognitive rational overlay presumes that people will do what they are told. If people are told to do something, rewarded for doing it or punished for not doing it, they will do it. This is the logic that underpins programs like the anti-AIDS campaigns. However, this is based on a logical model of human behavior and does not account for the emotional desire to hurt oneself or others, or feelings that one is worthless or powerless, except as a pathological condition despite the rampant escalation in targeted behaviors. Take the example of AIDS. Massive advertisement and public education about the dangers of unsafe sex and how to have safe sex have emerged in recent years, accelerating around 1985 after the death of Rock Hudson. Since then several trends have been noted. A sizable proportion of persons still practice unsafe sex, even among well-educated groups. The fastest growing group of HIV-positive persons is heterosexual women. Prostitution now advertises a new and more expensive service: "unsafe sex." None of this appears logical. It is however patterned, hence predictable if we take on a model of emotion that allows for an amplification of intervention stimuli, often opposite to the intended direction.

SUPRARATIONALITY

Suprarationality denotes my reference to emotion as a characteristic
of human groups that is above or beyond rationality.

This sets up a range of properties that can be modeled in and of their own right without reliance on a model of rationality. The central features of this model are emotion as (1) a property of context, (2) higher order, (3) nonlinear, and (4) equifinal or multifinal. This at once begins mapping out the property of emotion in human groups and separates it from other characteristics like meaning, cognition, and communication, in that emotion is the only one that is appropriately described by all four features.

Adding emotion to a wholes approach is a more complete representation, in the sense that it captures a greater range of the phenomena of human groups than has previously been done within a general systems theory approach. This lies in the observation that a conception of emotion allows for explanation of a greater range of human phenomena and incorporates basic systems theory notions. The human characteristic of emotion brings to life ideas like nonsummativity and equi- or multifinality. My sense is that a wholes approach that models emotion, though begun here with human groups, will lead to a revision of general systems theory approaches to a greater range of phenomena. I elaborate below four basic anchors of emotion as a characteristic of human groups that can guide investigation of other phenomena and may lead to exploration of emotion in other species or natural phenomena. Why assume humans are unique, even if this is our reference point?

Context-Level Emotion

It occurred to me while writing the section on nonsummativity that emotion plays out the principle of nonsummativity to a degree other characteristics cannot. The whole is greater than the sum of its parts. But where and what is the composition of this whole? Words, meanings, and communication can be viewed as co-emergent, but cognition or rationality is less amenable to being viewed as a whole. We can imagine groups having shared signals, a secret language, but is there such a thing as thinking as a unit? I offer that a cognitive rational model, especially where it relies on a mechanical or physiological view of thinking and intelligence and is underpinned by reliance on individual units bounded by skin, or fur, cannot use nonsummativity as its point of departure.

Emotion can. People in groups can feel as a unit and have co-emergent sadness, anger, disappointment, and so on, in ways in which they do not have collective thought. I offer that the principle of nonsummativity can be used to model human groups as exhibiting the characteristic of shared emotion. Perhaps it is possible to begin thinking in terms of "we-motions."

Higher Order

> "I can't. I'm in the depths of despair. Can you eat when you are in the depths of despair?"
>
> "I've never been in the depths of despair, so I can't say," responded Marilla.
>
> "Weren't you? Well, did you ever try to imagine you were in the depths of despair?"
>
> "No, I didn't."
>
> "Then I don't think you can understand what it's like. It's a very uncomfortable feeling indeed. When you try to eat a lump comes right up in your throat and you can't swallow anything, not even if it was a chocolate caramel. . . ."
>
> (Montgomery, 1908, p. 28)

This quote from *Anne of Green Gables* demonstrates the idea that emotion is a higher order or central property because it overrides other properties. The ability to move, become sexually aroused, think, find something, or swallow may all be impeded or improved by feelings. I have experienced this myself when I have lost my way going to a class that I have gone to twice a week for three months, or have accidentally shifted into first gear, rather than fourth gear, while upset. Tomkins allowed for this possibility in modeling all other physiological systems as secondary to the affect system (1981). Emotion can be thought of as overriding various forms of human behavior, an on/off or circuit interrupter switch that may forestall or amplify all other processes.

Nonlinear

Emotion can be seen as a characteristic that does not necessarily exhibit linear cause and effect sequences. It is with the property of nonlinearity that emotion breaks away from meaning and communication. While meaning and communication are contextual, they are also linear in the sense that they can be modeled as directly linked to systems of logic in contexts. A paralogical view of meanings sets up this principle in terms of judgment and interpretation but does not move in the direction of explaining why and how mental illness patienting begins and is driven. I offer that the core of this process lies in a property that can co-emerge in context in suprarational fashion, emotion.

Feelings can emerge or co-emerge in patterns that are not linear or finite. Emotions can begin from within a context, without external stimuli, and mushroom or disappear as rapidly as they co-emerged. A sideways glance at a potential sexual partner, caught by a current partner, can set off a wave of violence or abruptly end feelings of love. This is a play-out of the principle of cybernetics, self-steering leading to patterns that are not modeled by linear cause and effect.

Equifinality and Multifinality

The notion of equifinality and multifinality that was discussed in the abstract earlier is crucial for modeling emotion. It gives a graphic image of how the characteristic of emotion plays out in human groups in terms of specific events that punctuate analysis. Emotion can be seen as an explosive and conversely dampening property of human groups that enters into behavior and, as such, explains the observed patterns of equifinality and multifinality. The message of the unpredictability of outcomes when only inputs are known is mirrored in the unpredictability of emotional responses.

Conventionally thought of as the purview of individuals, emotions as context-level group traits can expand the explanatory power of models by looking not just at the individually manifested emotional response but at its emotional context. When one person becomes agitated and violent, is there a correlate in self-deprecating behavior in another part of the context?

The importance of this four-component model of emotion was driven home to me in the observation of videotapes of couples interacting. One case of a man and woman showed instances where the woman hit the man to get him to do what she instructed. Later in the interaction he responded nastily to her. This suggested to me that the emotional context as a whole was very brittle. Since both persons acted violently toward one another at different times, there was little point in trying to cast the emotion of violence in one person or the other. I therefore started looking instead at the emotional context as a whole and began to see a pattern of isolation and control that co-emerged with frustration and violence by both parts. Ultimately this led to a two-pole model of types of emotional patterns, that were more (definitional deficit) and conversely less (definitional equality) likely to lead to defining a family member as sick (Hanson, 1989a), as explained in greater detail in the next section.

By fleshing out four components of a model of emotion, it is possible to begin giving form to the more diffuse notion of feelings. I discussed above the concept that purchasing behavior can be fruitfully modeled as an emotional phenomenon. Giving the dimensions of context, centrality, cybernetics, and equifinality and multifinality gives directions for the hunt for predictions. What forms a context such that buying behavior can be predicted? What overrides cognition? Perhaps appealing to the frustrations of body changes in middle age with crash diets, electronic toners, and hair dyes leads to overriding cognition, and hence to massive product sales.

Time and again social policy has foundered where emotion has not been considered. Using a cognitive rational overlay has fallen short in explaining individual events on the case level. Assuming that spousal violence can be overcome by pointing out a series of costs and benefits to persons in the context is not likely to dig out the more centrally deterministic emotional roots of the relationship that manifest on the surface as violence. I argue that a phenomenon that is not reasonable to begin with cannot be reasoned away. Unless it is modeled as emotional, suprarational, there is little hope that the targeted behavior will stop.

The conception of suprarationality has four components that place emotion above and beyond rationality: context, centrality, cybernetics, and equifinality and multifinality. It is my own derivation (Hanson, 1991b). To form this conception I applied the systems notions of nonsummativity, feedback, and unpredictability, and linked them with Tomkins' (1981) notion of the centrality of affect. In sum, this model provides a better application of systems thinking in human groups than has been previously modeled and pulls emotion away from the realm of the individual unit and with it physiological explanations.

As contrary as contextual emotion is to the conventional views of emotion, seeing this as a characteristic of groups composed of parts other than humans may be even more so. Moving to a notion of suprarationality allows separation of human behavior from the behaviorist, cognitive rational models that were grounded in the assumed equivalence of humans with other species, most often rodents. At the same time, however, it suggests rethinking our models of other species. If we can mark out a new territory for human characteristics above and beyond rationality, it may be possible to do so with other species and physical phenomena. How does rodent task performance vary when it is done in groups, right after mating, after the death of an offspring? Are there nonlinear redundancies in physical systems like computers? If not, does this mean that artificial intelligence is impossible? Following this, it may be then possible to return to humans and consider what is at the heart of intelligence. Is it linear, as conventionally conceived, or emotional? Why do we speak of getting to the heart of things rather than the brain?

Suprarationality is a theoretical transcendence of models of rationality, as expanded by the four components of a model of emotion. This simultaneously gives form to an uncharted human characteristic and opens up territory for the discovery of other such traits. A colleague, after reading the journal version of my argument (Hanson, 1991b), asked if there were other things that could be modeled along the same dimensions as emotion. It occurred to me that spirituality is a possibility, but I have not worked on this and invite others to add to the list begun with emotion.

Doing research based on suprarationality is initially complex and confusing, but I suspect ultimately simpler. A conception of contextual emotion is complex and demands rethinking all aspects of research design and analysis that I have just begun (Hanson, 1991b, 1994e, in press-a, in press-b). Nonlinearity, co-emergence, and flexibility are all traits that are not generally witnessed in conventional data collection or statistical procedures. For the time being this necessitates running an investigation and analysis of research methodology simultaneously with any substantive pursuit. This is an extraordinarily complex process as it is necessary to begin rethinking statistical assumptions and applications as well as allowing for the dynamics that co-emerge in the research context itself. The payoff lies in seeing that while this is an onerous task, by going after a higher order property, the potential exists, if captured, for explaining a wider array of lower order behavior like meaning and communication; this would be similar to capturing the command center of a military operation.

I am prompted to offer that feeling is as legitimate, if not more so, than thinking in everyday life. I sense there is comfort and self-assurance that can be drawn from allowing one's feelings to be relevant and important, as much or more so than one's thoughts and rational arguments. Though the cast of convention may suggest eschewing emotion in favor of rationality, it is possible to think about what is important in one's own life and contexts of intimacy. Where do emotions like confidence, depression, or pride fit? In this way can we see our feelings as accomplishments.

DEFINITIONAL DEFICIT
AND DEFINITIONAL EQUALITY

Definitional deficit and definitional equality are poles of a model
of emotional patterns in contexts that capture emotional gapping
versus sharing. As such they model contexts that are more
(deficit) and conversely less (equality) likely to correlate
with the process of defining a family member as sick.

I present the definitional deficit, definitional equality typology, as an example of a theory that can be built within a wholes approach drawing on suprarationality. It provides two rough poles of emotional patterns in families. The use of "definition" in each of the patterns derives from my observation that the process of defining in context is driven by deeper emotional patterns. I provide here only a brief of the typology, and refer readers who are interested to the detailed presentation of my ideas in *The Intimate Politics of Sense* (Hanson, 1994a) or "Definitional deficit: A model of senile dementia in context" (Hanson, 1989a).

The target definition that focused my model-building was mental illness in family contexts. In particular I observed videotaped interaction samples of 45 families with aged members, some of whom (29) were identified as senile dementia patients. This allowed watching for patterns in families that were more or less likely to be correlated with the construction and maintenance of the idea that someone was sick.

Taking a realities stance prompted me to discard notions of sanity and insanity as universals and to look instead at how abnormality was constructed in context. This meant doing an analysis of the interaction samples without knowing which families had identified patients and which did not, as diagnosed by Dr. George Neiderehe and Dr. Ernest Fruge (1984). After extensive viewing of the tapes and various attempts at coding, the deficit–equality separation began to surface.

I saw patterns in some cases where ostensible evidence of mental illness like forgetfulness was not considered a problem, where in others the same behavior was problematic. I also saw patterns where evidence of illness was constructed by a systematic process of setting up and trapping the aged family member. As I began to look deeper than these surface meaning and communication patterns, it became clear that there were emotional overriders to the linear surface behaviors. In cases where there was a patient, it seemed that this patient was constantly considered wrong, sick, or inappropriate, because they never participated in the ongoing process of constructing what passed for reality, sense, or truth. It was not so much that they *did not* know what was real, but rather that they *could not* know what was real.

The construction of the idea that something was wrong with someone seemed to be tied to an emotional pattern in the context as a whole whereby emotional ties were somehow clogged in total and not shared by the person considered sick. In this way subtle messages about shifts in what is going on, say from humor to criticism, were missed by the patient. The whole family seemed to be in distress and focused their feelings on one person as the explanation for what was wrong, why everyone was upset and uncomfortable. I came to call this form of emotional pattern of uneven connections *definitional deficit*. It reflects how deficits in terms of emotional connections are translated into surface patterns, like defining a family member as mentally ill.

It is important to remember a key lesson of a wholes approach: BLAME IS A NON SEQUITUR. The pattern does not appear deliberate or even conscious on the part of any family member, either the isolated patient or those controlling the definitions. If anything it seems at times that distress is greatest for the controller(s).

In sharp contrast, definitional equality reflects contexts where emotional connections are wide open and shared equally. There may be massive overt conflict and argument, but people agree to disagree and the emotional distress that accompanies disagreement dissipates. This is in direct opposition to deficit contexts where anger lingers because there is no way to have a head-on fight. Contentious issues are avoided or redefined for the person raising them. The equality context looks bouncy and flexible, while the deficit context is brittle and rigid.

In total the two types represent contexts where it is less, deficit, and conversely more, equality, likely that changes or new stimuli will lead to distress and with it the definition of problems or pathological conditions. Mental illness in intimate relations is one kind of problem that comes to be constructed in this way. It is also possible to think about other types of contexts and what forms of change or new stimuli may lead to the construction of problems or not. Here the relevance of the deficit–equality typology will be relevant in relation to the degree of emotional involvement in a context as mediated by the duration of the relationship.

The current economic recession is fertile ground for exploring the concept of deficit and equality in businesses. Here I would look into which businesses are surviving the recession and which others have folded. I sense it is possible to use my typology to look at the emotional patterns in business contexts that may explain their ability to adapt to changes in the economic environment. It is possible to look at how similar organizations reacted to initial disruptions like climbing interest rates.

I would predict that in a context of deficit there would be immediate attempts to attribute concurrent declining profits or projects running out of financing to the failings of one or a few people. These people would be degraded and or laid off along with others in lower-level clerical and service positions. This would increase levels of fear and insecurity among other staff who would begin to curtail risky behavior such as coming up with creative solutions or providing new ideas on what to do. Those who feel confident in themselves and have the skills to succeed elsewhere would go to other businesses or start their own, depleting the high quality resources of the business and increasing the quality of their competition. As such it would lead to a spiraling downward trend for the organization.

Contrarily in an equality context, problems would not be personalized. Individuals would be allowed to make mistakes without reprisal because they are valued members of the organization, secure in the knowledge that ultimately creativity and innovation pays off. Instead of layoffs, all levels of staff would participate in coming up with strategies for adapting to change and would decide to take a short term across the board wage freeze. New ventures would be tried. Staff members with new ideas would come over from deficit organizations where they were afraid to make suggestions. In total, I suggest the deficit equality typology may provide a model that could be applied to organizations other than intimate relations, in recognition that at least some of the dynamics, particularly as regard emotional reactions, are relevant.

The lesson in social policy is to watch for the surface reaction of scapegoating particular individuals or parts of a system in order to explain and intervene in targeted problems. In the same way emotional distress leads to focusing on a family member as THE PROBLEM, it may lead to targeting a member of the system rather than looking at the dynamics of the context as a whole that made such a definition inevitable. Relevant examples here are Richard Nixon with Watergate and Ben Johnson with sports drug use. In both cases the act of the individual became the focus and, as such, THE PROBLEM, even as it became clear that the so-called problem behaviors were common practice in the systems in question. This effectively focused attention away from the distressing patterns in the system and ensured that they continue. In the case of Watergate, my sense is that this initial evidence of scandal or crime in government worked somewhat like inoculation, paving the way for the acceptance of even greater degrees of corruption, as evidenced by the "Iran-Contra" investigations. As with mental illness, a deficit context, acted upon in terms of the publicly offered explanation, will likely serve to maintain and even escalate the stated problem. The deficit equality typology thus becomes a means of separating out forms of contexts in order to intervene more effectively and with less likelihood of worsening a targeted problem.

The derivations of the typology are the theoretical constructs of a wholes approach developed in interaction with my empirical experience with the dynamics of intimacy. Seeing emotion as a higher order property, as in the analysis of senile dementia, allows us to get at a central feature that explains other lower-level manifestations. Use of a wholes approach means that models derived via analysis of intimate relations can be transported intact to other types of relations, be it corporate or political. The dynamics of intimacy are more readily amenable to wholes-grounded analysis in that they are easier to observe directly, and thus provide a profitable ground for developing models that have much wider applicability, as I will discuss in greater detail in the next section on content and context.

The definitional deficit–definitional equality typology is relevant theoretically in its own right as a substantive map of how emotional patterns play out in surface behaviors in intimate relations. As such it challenges models that define conflict in families as pathological. It is also significant theoretically as an illustration of a model developed within a wholes approach. All the outlined basics of a general systems theory approach in combination with a constructivist view of human group behavior are respected by the typology. At the same time a specific substantive area, mental illness and intimacy, is fleshed out. As such it provides an exemplar for other substantive models.

For research, guidance is given as to how to decode raw data, such as video-taped interaction samples, in terms of a model with emotion as its central property. It is possible to read surface manifestations as projections of a deeper pattern by looking at meaning, interaction, and communication in sequence to detect emotional patterns in the context. Once the theoretical suggestion that the surface is driven by the roots is accepted, it is possible to begin fitting these surface projections until a model of the root appears.

In personal terms it is possible to think about forms of targeted behavior and whether or not it may be masking pain that is experienced more generally and intensified rather than relieved by focusing it on a target. Do you try to hurt or degrade others who are close to you when you are feeling rejected or ineffectual? The saying "misery loves company" may be a truism that reflects this and can guide understanding of where the move to define others as a problem is centered.

CONTEXT AND CONTENT— LIGHT THROUGH A PRISM

Emotional contexts are refracted into social contents like light through a prism. This can explain different individual events under like structural conditions.

The characteristic of emotion can be used to bring together and set in motion a wholes approach to human behavior. In the first chapter of this section, I laid the groundwork for a context and content separation, representing the basics of a general systems theory approach and the specific properties of human group interaction, notably meaning and communication. The importance of this separation lies in going beyond explanations that only go as far as average tendencies in populations. It makes it possible to begin modeling the crucial question, "Why one and not another, under like structural conditions?"

I offer that emotion is a characteristic that can explain which case exhibits that form of behavior when linked to a general systems theory approach as outlined in this book. Approximating these separations in observed behavior requires a concept of emotion in that any given instance of human behavior needs to be modeled with an emotional component. Furthermore, this component needs be modeled along the lines of a systems approach, minimally as regards nonsummativity, and preferably adding ideas like cybernetics and equi- and multifinality.

This move to emotion is justified both metatheoretically and substantively. In terms of the structure of theory, a wholes approach with a suprarational conceptualization of emotion provides a better behavior trap in that the model is a better fit for human behavior. By seeing emotionality as a central feature of human behavior, one that is nonlinear and contextual, the restrictive overlay of rationality on emotion is transcended. A new map for understanding targeted behaviors is provided by pointing out different paths on which to look both historically and pro-actively. Instead of looking merely in straight lines and for individual points, a greater range of possibilities is suggested. Link spousal abuse today to anorexia yesterday and alcoholism tomorrow, instead of to spousal abuse yesterday and tomorrow.

The context and content separation, as part of a wholes approach, allows for considering events in processes rather than targeted products. Shifting away from linear and into cybernetic causality means that a specific targeted behavior becomes a conceptual punctuation point for analysis, rather than the assumed model of the phenomena. We target an event of interest, assuming that this is our decision for purposes of analysis rather than a causal representation. This need to freeze or dissect is an analytic technique. If the phenomenon is conceived of as a process, but measured as a sum of products, it is never seen as a process; instead, it is inferred. This is perhaps a fine, but nevertheless crucial, distinction. It must constantly be remembered that how we see influences what we see. To see wholes we must allow for wholes in the way we see.

Taking the context and content separation into motion, after being reminded of process epistemology through a focus on events, means setting aside the alleged level debate that is rooted in linear causality. Instead attention is paid to the back and forth rhythm of human group process, the interphase between the dynamics of intimate contexts and social contents. To illustrate this new form of approach, I shall present a model of the patienting process in mental illness as one type of substantive issue that illuminates the nature of social processes.

Like light through a prism, the dynamics of intimacy that lead to a move to define someone as sick are refracted into the age and gender contents of a particular social context. The process of "patienting" begins and is driven by intimate contexts. This central on/off switch and directional control, seated in emotional patterns, is at the heart of the move to seek patient status. Once contact is made with clinical contexts, this process in intimacy that is diffuse and a characteristic of the emotional context as a whole becomes focused on individuals rather than contexts. Furthermore, there is a move to fit the patterns of intimate context as a whole onto a specific individual as a part, in terms of this part's age and gender. Because of this the person chosen to be a patient in intimate context may change if he or she does not fit available categories. Over time this means that a single context-level pattern of emotional distress may manifest in varying age and gender pairings and changing membership. In this sense a single case of emotional distress will appear as a series of unconnected individual illnesses over time with no means of seeing these parts as a whole. Furthermore, this constant refraction may exacerbate the degree of distress in intimate contexts by taking away stated explanations and forcing a constant search for new ones.

Reliance on the content of age and gender categories, in the mode of summative causality as a path to average tendencies, completely misses the contextual separation of distressed versus nondistressed intimate contexts that might explain case level events in the patienting process. If the sum of aggregate prevalence of some targeted condition is used as the reference for explanation, it is doomed to fail in that the unit of interest is never allowed into the data set. A wholes approach suggests making such linkages using intimate contexts as the reference unit and given individual manifest conditions as events in patienting processes that are centered in the emotions of intimate relations. In this way it will be possible to clear away the distractions created by focusing on conditions as outcomes or products and see instead the more crucial roots upon which individual conditions are mere surface growths.

Imagine the difference if we shift from thinking about categories as deterministic, as is the tendency of linear causality, to categories as diagnostic. The process of categorization itself comes into focus. Sexist and racist attitudes that may prevail in a social context are not shown by all members of that context. Why not? To focus on the refraction alone, expressed sexism or racism, misses the dynamics of what leads to this person acting one way while another does not. This seems particularly important when elimination of sexism and racism is a goal. Here the dynamics of feminism and antiracism would seem crucial to investigate.

A focus on process through events, rather than products through categories, opens up a range of possibilities. The surface projection of spouse abuse as coded into a system that reads this emotional context distress as a question of individual problems as coded by age and gender—wife abuse, granny bashing—will miss the central feature of emotion that drives the process. If an individual is blamed in the categories appropriate for a social context, there is no way of seeing the context of his or her behavior over time, and because of this there is no way of changing the roots of the distress.

In business contexts it may be worthwhile to remind ourselves that we cannot confuse the product with the process. A focus on the product, for instance low efficiency ratings, as THE PROBLEM will miss the underlying roots of distress that may be projecting this. Focus on the product and intervention to alter the product, if it is merely an outgrowth of low self-esteem promoted by top-down management, may mean that a new growth shoots up. Efficiency ratings increase, but so do sick days, or staff resign to go elsewhere.

Changing a product in social process via policy can only be effective if a wholes approach is used. Otherwise, it is bound to exacerbate the situation. Various attempts in the last 15 years to prevent and turn around economic recession present an example. Even though the recession that bottomed out in 1981 co-emerged with high interest rates and high unemployment, a policy of high interest rates was again introduced in the late 1980s. Another recession was spawned at the beginning of the 1990s. The policy of high interest rates was later reversed to point that interest rates in 1994 were approximately half what they were in 1991. However, fear and trepidation created by these financially disastrous cycles and fueled by vacillating policies remained. Businesses and consumers spent little and were fearful of long-term financial commitments. Here, the influence of interest rates in process becomes impossible to predict based on the act of raising or lowering alone. Looking at a single product like spending as finite misses the tendency of a system to act in unpredictable ways given its ability to steer and self-regulate.

Putting context and content in motion with the image of refraction of intimate process into social content is in essence the extension of all the ideas dealt with earlier in this book. It presents my summary model of social processes as grounded in the basics of a general systems theory approach with assumptions about human meaning, communication, and emotion added in order to flesh out substantive issues.

As such this presents a new model of social process that allows for motion and expansion into various other forms of phenomena. Though I have couched my discussion in terms of the optional addition of assumptions about human characteristics, this does not mean the derivations can only be used to study human groups. Quite the contrary, the derivations of a general systems approach mean that the theory in total or any of its components can be transported for use to any kind of phenomena that meets the systems point of departure that the whole is greater than the sum of its parts.

Research is directed by the image of refraction to get away from surface projections either as targets or as products. My model suggests both that this is not the appropriate target, contexts are, and that focus on outcomes straight-jackets the process in ways that render it inexplicable. Because of this, tech-niques based on linear causality and aggregate analysis are inappropriate. The assumptions of existing techniques need to be rethought within a whole episte-mology, or if found wanting, replaced with new, more fitting techniques.

In everyday experience it may be possible to think about our own tendency to respond in categories as cause. Are we too quick to allow the social content of category to frame our own contextually centered emotions? Do we resort to sexist and racist categories in response to our own feelings of insecurity, unat-tractiveness, or disillusionment? The refraction message here is that such cate-gories, because they are only surface outgrowths of more deeply rooted anxi-eties, are bound to disappoint as an explanation for our own feelings of distress. Resort to such categories may even amplify our distress as the category neither explains nor relieves pain, but because there is no way to see the roots of the pain, the category is reinforced.

Chapter 8

Moving Ahead

I have presented stories of Aristotle, Alice, and Anne. Aristotle gave us the notion of nonsummativity. Alice showed how meaning is specific to context. Anne made emotion as a higher order human characteristic clear.

The question of where to go with a wholes approach requires stepping back and forward. I have argued various ways under different headings that a general systems theory approach is something that may be known intuitively, yet not captured in formal ways of knowing. The epistemology of a wholes approach is one which attempts to step back from modes of observation and analysis that may restrict phenomena in ways that render them inexplicable.

It may be the assumptions of conventional epistemology such as linear causality, summative math, and rationality that make it impossible to explain any more than a minor proportion of human behavior. This failure is in the conventional model itself in that it imposes a view of human behavior rooted in ideological beliefs about how humans ought to be. By imposing rationality as the guiding frame, humans are found wanting, imperfect, diseased. A wholes approach, especially as it allows for emotion, promises to get past this trap. Rather than apply an idealized view of human rationality, a model of human emotionality is allowed for. A model based on rationality will be relevant only as far as human beings act rationally. I ask, how much of human behavior is rational? I offer that human behavior is less rational than it is emotional. Moves to rationalize human behavior emerge from a desire to impose rationality as a preferred image rather than from effective modeling. Rationality may please, but it does not fit.

It is thus with emotion that a wholes approach provides its most radical break with convention. The basics of a general systems theory approach like nonsummativity, cybernetics, feedback, and so on, which I outline in this book in detail, have been around for some time, although they have not penetrated the social and behavioral sciences. To the best of my knowledge, these constructs have not yet been used to ground a model of emotion in human groups.

I suspect the addition of an epistemology of emotion might be possible in the context of feminist analysis. Ideas of reason have proliferated and been found wanting for the analysis of women. I argue that this failure of a model of reason was an imposition of the preferred image of men. Because of this it has failed in the analysis of women and men. The straight jacket of reason has bound the expressiveness and creativity of emotion, and with it the individuals who are trapped in gender categories that restrict and deny a whole range of experience.

To go ahead, it is not enough to attack surface projections of epistemology; the roots must be dug out. To add women into the model of ideal men is as unfitting for women as it is for men. The problems of inexplicability project as an inability to reflect women's experience. They are, however, rooted in deeper foundations that attempt to restrict and reduce human experience rather than understand its totality. By denying emotion, models deny humanness, and as such are bound to fail in capturing it.

Epistemological problematics that arise from notions of linearity, summativity, and rationality, are bound to disappoint in the study of human behavior because this approach is like trying to capture fish with tweezers. We assume the phenomena is a certain form, then go after it with the logical tool. When we fail to capture it in total, just tear off pieces (which may make things worse) rather than try a new type of tool, we build bigger tweezers. However, unless the model fits the phenomena, and tools appropriate to the tasks are derived, it will be a disappointing search.

In this vein the challenges to feminist analysis that have come from women of color were inevitable. While changing the conclusions and derivations of conventional epistemology, feminist analysis has yet to alter the epistemology itself. This process has begun with the work of Dorothy Smith (1987).

I add to this by offering that the spirit of feminist analysis is in essence epistemological. This spirit can be freed from the traps of convention by entering into a different mode of theorizing. Instead of resorting to canon (feminist theory), a plural approach is needed: feminisms (feminist theories). Unless this is done challenges like the recent ones from women of color are inevitable. The search for canon itself must be challenged by a move to a multiversal, rather than universal, conception, else the whole point of feminisms be lost. This is the essence of a realities view.

Finding *the way*, one that excluded women, has been critiqued extensively by feminist authors in that *the way* was men's way. Authors who then proceed to offer that their way, *the feminist way*, is *the way*, are as prone to their own original criticism as was man-centered theory. I argue that, although this projects as an issue of men's and women's theory, it is more fundamentally a projection of nomotheism, which makes inevitable challenges in terms of whose reality is real.

It was not just the white, middle-class nature of feminism that led to the challenge from women of color, but rather the search for canon itself as an offshoot of logical positivism. No matter which reality is considered real it will ultimately fail to explain, if singular. This is where I see the spirit of feminism.

The idea that one group's reality was excluded from conventional versions of reality suggests examining the dynamics of exclusion, rather than just revising the version of reality. I offer that implicit or explicit reliance on logical positivist epistemology is such a dynamic, one that can be transcended by a wholes approach. It allows for feminism, but not just feminism. As such it is a more inclusive theoretical approach and, because of this, a better representation of the spirit of feminism, one which will hold up better to challenge than the alleged single feminist canon.

SCIENCE

Science can be thought of as the refinement of theory.

This means that refinement depends on the theory in question. I discuss the idea of science in terms of a wholes approach as it opens up modes of inquiry, as novel as the basics of a systems approach and my additions regarding characteristics of human groups. The central point here is that science in its most basic form is not necessarily equivalent to logical positivism. In practice it may have come to pass that the notion of science is directly equivalent to the dictates of logical positivism. This is not necessarily true. Furthermore, it is not the only possible mode of science. Multiverse, emotion, and subjectivity are as legitimate cornerstones for science as are universalism, logic, and objectivity. The refinement of theories within either set is guided by fit between inquiry and concepts. Therefore the methods for use with a wholes approach can be developed in terms of the approach's own theoretical cornerstones without falling back on the traditional techniques of logical positivism. Science within a wholes approach requires rethinking the basis of knowledge and finding proof at each turn.

Multiverse

Conceiving of human experience as situated in contexts with their own inherent basis for legitimacy means speaking in terms of multiverse rather than universe. This means using language like "human experience" rather than "the world," and plurals like realities, contexts, wisdoms, and so on. The relevance of this lies in altering the discourse of science to reflect a wholes approach in order that such discourse not be constrained by the language of an inappropriate conceptual scheme. This is seen in the use of impersonal voice, "It was discovered," to be implied collective in terms such as "they say," or "we conclude," even when there is only one concluder.

To recall the discussion of realities, the imperative is to strive for and present in terms of *a way* rather than *the way.* Success becomes defined in terms of how well a refined model fits a particular context rather than on its representation of general trends in a population.

The grounds for this radical shift in thinking comes from the principle of nonsummativity, which makes relational wholes of two or more parts the unit of analysis. Rather than an alleged population parameter to approximate, the unit becomes the context of interest, however defined. Thus, fit rather than representativeness becomes the basis for judging research conclusions.

A wholes approach suggests that using science in terms of the particular and contextual as the target unit will ultimately lead to a better approximation of the total phenomena than will using the general and acontextual as the target unit. Rather than drill out context specificity in the name of universalism and objectivity, these unique variations become the focus of analysis. Therefore analysis will go farther toward achieving validity at the case level. If one conceives of a phenomenon as co-emergent, contextual, and subjective, and researches it as such, the chances for measuring what we think we are measuring are better. Rather than acontextual generalization as a means of communicating significance of findings, abstraction to principle and pattern as focused on the context becomes the goal. In essence this means doing less reduction of phenomena in the process of collecting data, and so enhances validity.

The result will be a number of models that fit contexts rather than a singular model that reflects the most frequent common trait. This means that although results will be more complex because they will be multiple, *ways* as opposed to *way,* the chances for explaining total variance are increased dramatically in that the entire data set is potentially explainable. Instead of looking for a central tendency or midpoint, we are able to look for a series of models that can fit all instances.

Emotion

The Final Frontier? I was intrigued by the Star Trek movie where the premise is that Mr. Spock has a brilliant half-brother who believed that it was in emotion, not logic, where the basis for wisdom lies. This is my inclination as well.

I muse as to whether drilling emotion out of science has been its salvation, as the positivists might claim. Or, has it limited science to the realm of physical phenomena and in so doing handicapped its ability to study human group behavior? It is possible that during the Enlightenment the desire to move science away from deity led to the denial or discard of emotion. As I previously discussed in detail, I argue that emotion has been noticeable by its absence from models of human behavior and I offer a model of emotion as an explosive or dampening central higher order characteristic of human group behavior, which overrides rationality, logic, and cognition. How is it possible to incorporate this model into a view of scientific inquiry?

The process of science may have been as much emotional as logical in terms of its biggest discoveries and shifts in thinking. I reject the notion of linearity that is implicit in Kuhn (1970) in favor of a model of multifinality, seated in emotion. Though the techniques of statistics, laboratory study, interviewing, and so on may be learned and practiced in a rote, linear fashion, I argue that these practices are not what lead to discovery, creation, and innovation. The discoverers of penicillin may have been looking at petri dishes of rotting food for months. What was it that piqued them to spot the original penicillin?

I am reminded of the story from *The Hitch Hiker's Guide to the Galaxy* (1979/1992) where it is recounted in the future that at one point on Earth they tried to discover the meaning of life. To do this a massive computer was built to house and analyze all known data. The computer churned away for years while the populace eagerly awaited its response. The answer it finally produced was "47." It was concluded that they would have to build another even bigger computer to figure out what that meant. I argue that while logic and linear accumulation and assessment of information may be part of the process of scientific advance, it is insufficient to capture any but the known derivations of information. Innovation rests on a leap into a parallogical scheme of interpretation, which may be triggered by human emotional responses that are not reducible to logic or cognition. Once leaps are made the process of reasoning may begin, but it cannot approximate the basis of reason in context. This makes it useful to take a parallogical view of science by transporting the tools of logic into particular contexts that may be based in, and shifted by, emotion.

Subjectivity

A subjective science is one where subjective impressions, constructions, and interpretations become the front and center focus of inquiry, rather than bias or noise to be drilled out. This means taking a model of human reflexive capabilities through every phase of the theory refinement process. In particular this means seeing scientists, as well as research subjects, as subjective humans in context.

It is possible to begin thinking about particular contextual meanings that emerge in the process of scientific analysis, which may be as relevant as conclusions about the targeted phenomena. For instance, in the course of collaborative work on intimate contexts and senile dementia, the investigators in Texas noticed an unusually high rate of illness among the research staff, and coping patterns from the research subjects wandering into the personal relationships of research staff. This was the initial clue to my modeling patterns of exclusion, which led to defining a family member as sick on the emotional level. The observation of illness patterns wandering into the lives of people who had no shared history or learned behaviors with these troubled families made me think about what could possibly be the channel for dispersion. Then I began to think about emotion because I could not see where a logical or cognitive explanation had any relevance. If a theory that is being refined defines subjectivity as a characteristic of human group behavior, then it seems relevant to allow for subjectivity in the study of human behavior. This means building impressions into the process of data collection and analysis directly.

TOOLS

Going forth with a wholes approach as outlined in this book in theoretical terms will also require thinking about methods. Having eschewed the approach of trying to capture fish with tweezers, I offer here some ideas about tools. This means thinking back to the abstract theoretical notions of a general systems theory approach and carrying them into practical strategies for doing research. I have organized some ideas around the headings of data, decoding, and general constructs.

Data

The first issue for me when thinking about research is to think about data—the relationship between the world and the views of the analyst. I offer that while we may conventionally think that the business of research is collecting information, which comes to be called data, we can also think of this as a process of reduction. Worlds of experience are vast; numbers of stimuli incalculable. To begin research is to somehow select what we are interested in from this vast pool.

Data can be seen as the process via which we move from the total world of experiences to the pieces selected for analysis. In this sense we are reducing from a total range to the specific information wanted for research. I have de-

marcated four issues, unit—sequence, time, and range—which bear on this reduction process within the ideas of a wholes approach.

Unit. I begin with unit as it is perhaps the most crucial issue for a wholes
approach in that it addresses its point of departure. If we accept that the whole
is greater than the sum of its parts, there are two methodological imperatives.
First, there must be wholes in our data. Second, you cannot find wholes by
summing parts.

This means two things in practical terms. At a minimum there must be wholes
of two interrelated parts in the data set. These two parts must be retained as a
relationship and cannot be inferred by reconstructing a relational piece of data
through any summative mathematical procedure.

In intimate relations this would mean seeing and collecting data on two spouses,
or a parent and child, together, rather than interviewing each separately and
then coming up with a relational score for happiness. Suppose an executive
notices that recent hiring decisions in her or his division seem to result in selecting less qualified candidates who contribute little to the job or resign within
the first year. An investigation strategy could meet the minimum criteria for
unit by observing hiring committee interactions, either by videotape or a researcher sitting in. Results may suggest that the interpersonal dynamics of the
group tend to lead to a lowest common denominator decision, a less qualified
but less controversial candidate. This would suggest an intervention strategy
whereby formal procedures for defining and assessing criteria were established
to govern decision making. A social policy strategy may be suggested by observing the dynamics of situations that lead to violence and aggression in gangs
to try to prevent it. Eyewitness accounts from individuals would be less effective than recordings of the events. In practical terms this could involve directing
existing security observations systems to research purposes.

Sequence. Cybernetic causality as an epistemological frame suggests attending to linked sequences of events. This means observing pieces one after
another, rather than at separated time points and inferring the linkages, and
keeping sequence units intact.

In intimate relations this would mean observing face-to-face interaction in
linked sequences of action-reaction-counteraction, rather than taking each phrase
and gesture unit as a piece, assigning it some value, then reconstituting the
relational pattern mathematically. The message of context is that such pieces
will not contain the co-emergent patterns of wholes. If sequences are taken
apart, then it will not be possible to find context. This issue became particularly
relevant in my own work on senile dementia in intimate contexts (Hanson, 1992)

when I saw the large degree of variability in terms of the number of gestures that went into the same pattern. Some families are louder and faster than others when arguing. Some talk more than others. This seemed to vary by cultural heritage. Had I presupposed what constituted a relevant phrase or gesture, I might have been led to reiterate cultural variations and missed the deeper emotional patterns that cut across cultures. It was necessary to watch continuous sequences of events within individual families, as well as across families in the data set, before I could spot similar emotional patterns as they manifested in different numbers of surface communications.

In an organization, the issue of sequence might be called into play by looking at the way decisions emerge at one point in time but are later reversed. I am reminded of the expression here that "the camel is a horse designed by a committee." To return to the question of hiring decisions, watch the total process whereby when discussing individual candidates the merits and weaknesses of each were agreed upon, yet the person recommended for the job is a candidate who has fewer strengths and more weaknesses than the other candidates. Knowledge of the points of decision on strengths and weaknesses would not sum up the decision to hire a weaker candidate. Finding a pattern to explain this co-emergent not logically summed decision would require viewing the whole sequence.

Consider the issue of mall-swarming, and how to prevent it. Imagine the difference between still-frame pictures versus a continuous sequence film. Not only might catalyst events be missed, there would be no means of seeing processes that did not sum into an outbreak of violence. Suppose there were two malls side by side and two gangs entered them. A swarming occurred in one but not the other. In both malls there was an initial event, like a gang member stealing a candy bar, but in one case the store owner talked to the thief and tried to reason with him or her, or just ignored it. In the other, police were called or the owner pulled out a gun or made threats. A sequential analysis might unearth patterns in the potential swarm that did not lead to the swarm event, compared with one that did, in order to guide policies for prevention.

Time. The issue of time is closely related to sequence, in that sequences take place in time, such that to see sequence means seeing time. I separate them here to suggest that sequence itself is not enough without time periods that allow observation of subsequent repetitions of the co-emergent pattern of interest. What this means is that any reduction process must proceed with extreme caution, especially initially, lest the time length piece be too small to capture the phenomena.

Reference to time in the issue of data is justified by both equi- and multifinality and suprarationality. In both cases the time dimension is crucial because errors can be made by assuming a linear relation between cause and effect. This is the essence of an emotional or suprarational stance, as modeled by equi- and multifinality. Without looking at a continuous time dimension, it may not be possible to see instances where in equifinal and multifinal fashion stimuli lead to the obverse of linear or rational causal linkages. Emotion may never be seen if there are no data that suggest this pattern of explosiveness or dampening in contexts that do not fit a model of reason.

In intimate relations research, I was confused initially by my observations of how ostensibly insane behavior was taken as sane and ostensibly sane behavior was taken as insane, in context. It was not until I was able to look at the full-time segments for each family that I began to detect patterns of emotional origin that overrode surface definitions of reason and cause, to the point that constructing insanity out of sanity was possible by a consistent pattern of exclusion and trapping until a definition of a person as sick was floated and maintained. Looking only at time points would have forced inference of disease pattern, in that these illogical cause and effect sequences would be inexplicable. Seeing events in time allowed for positing a pattern of emotion that could render the illogical explicable.

For the corporate hiring example, the suggestion would be to look for emerging emotional patterns, such as coalitions based on fear of the threats presented by an extremely competent, hence high achieving, person. Over time it would be possible to observe the pattern whereby persons expressing support for the most competent candidate are denied credibility in the process of decision making such that persons with unclear opinions are swayed to support the lesser qualified candidate. New reasons emerge that were not presented in the original consideration of candidates; individual decisions are based on irrelevant criteria. A continuous time segment would allow looking at how a process began based on one principle, assessment relative to criteria, and mutated into another, personal preference based on emotional patterns.

Research on mall-swarming might look at the emotional patterns that emerge in specific gangs. It may be that two gangs of similar structural makeup, age, class, race, or gender, have very different emotion patterns such that an instigating incident in one leads to blowing off steam in the group and a return to emotional calm, while in the other it erupts into violence directed toward the gang members, outsiders, or physical objects. By observing different gangs over time it would be possible to chart the dynamics of emotional reactivity and its results in ways that inferring structural cause could not explain. Inferences about structure would be complemented by continuous time observations. The ability to explain individual case level events within the broader rubric of structure would be enhanced. It may be observed that gangs' tendencies are typified by certain structural characteristics of race, age, gender, or class. This does not, however, explain why some gangs become violent while others do not. Being careful with time in the process of reduction to data may thus increase the degree of explanation in structurally oriented theories. Through this a means may be found of counteracting ageism, sexism, and racism.

Range. By range I refer to the number of different kinds of information that become data. This would involve what kinds of behavior are (1) seen, (2) recorded, and (3) analyzed. Possibilities for types of information are verbal and nonverbal behavior, actual behavior versus self-reported behavior, impressions, and observations. These spring to mind for the analysis of human behavior in groups from a wholes approach, but the possible range is endless.

Looking at verbal as well as nonverbal behavior is justified both by a dual model of communication, report and command, and by the model of suprarationality. If either communication or emotional patterns are to be discerned, it must be possible to see not just people's words, but their facial expressions and body movements. In my own work this became crucial in terms of watching for instances when a verbal exchange between a couple would lead to one spouse shaking, manifesting a symptom of Parkinson's disease. In a managerial setting this might mean looking not just at what people say in a meeting but looking into their eyes, or reviewing the speaking order to see if someone who generally has excellent ideas is conforming to those of his or her boss for political reasons. Working on a policy on affirmative action might involve getting together with senior administrators and junior women in an institution and watching the dynamics whereby women are allowed or not allowed to participate. Does the president ask a women for an opinion, then turn to a colleague to share a private remark while she is speaking? In each case it is useful to examine both verbal and nonverbal behavior to unearth wholes that are at the center of behavior but may not surface in verbal exchanges.

Actual behavior and reported behavior is particularly relevant to conception of realities or multiverse. The message of these ideas is that human contexts will have meaning sets that are specific to them. This makes it tenuous to rely solely on reports of what is going on from people involved in the context. It also makes it valuable to have both reports about what is going on and data on actual behavior in order to compare the two. This has been helpful in my work on mental illness where I was able to see verbal reports from one family member about how sick the patient member was, while at the same time observing how the alleged patient seemed to have a clear grasp and gave more accurate responses than did the reporting member. In a corporate setting it would be possible to collect data on what people did as well as what they said they did. Suppose a committee chair said he or she made sure that all committee members had a chance to express opinions, but in fact interrupted persons with opinions contradictory to his or her own, or only allowed certain people to speak after a consensus had been reached. A policy-directed investigation might compare forms filled out that say that an institution is acting correctly in terms of all the dictates of a policy on affirmative action for women, with the organization's actual hiring rate of two men for every one woman. In this dimension it is not just having the two types of data, reports and actual behavior, but the opportunities for comparison that they present that is useful.

It is important for the ideas of meaning and emotion that impressions be included along with observations in the range of data collected. People, both research subjects and research staff, can be encouraged to include not just observations, "I saw," but impressions that tap feelings, gut impressions, intuition, or uncertainties. This includes data on subjective meaning as well as contextual emotion in a data set in ways that are not possible in conventional approaches that triangulate qualitative and quantitative data, but ultimately fail because they are not comparable. I have tried a new strategy in my own work by collecting impression data along with formal data on coding procedures in the same data collection process. In practical terms this meant doing codes for dimensions of a formal model and for impressions such as liking, being comfortable, and so on. I have been delighted by the results thus far because it is possible to argue based on the results that these impression data are as good, if not better, predictors of focus dimensions like whether or not there is a senile dementia patient in the case (Hanson, in press-b). In an organization this could be addressed by collecting data not just on observations like productivity but impressions like feelings of confidence, insecurity, fun, or dedication. In social policy this strategy has been used to get at the subjective dimensions of sexism and racism that influence how people achieve, but are not detectable through conventional observations about IQ, education, or management skills. Concepts like "chilly climate" and "sloped playing field" have come out of this tradition.

Decoding

Decoding refers to how information is fitted to theories. This is grounded in the basic notion of validity as the fit between theory and method, or whether or not we are measuring what we think we are measuring. For a wholes approach this can be seen as a constant co-emergent feedback process between data and models. Data drive models. Models drive data. Within a wholes approach the two are as inseparable as parts from a whole, the notion that founds the approach.

The specifics of a wholes approach suggest that the legitimacy of analysis can be justified relative to a notion of multiverse. Rejecting a notion of universe in favor of multiverse means that the criteria of external or universal significance, or as it comes to mean in practice, degree of approximation, is inappropriate. Instead the locus of judgment becomes specific to the context of the theory being refined.

Each scientist or person who seeks to refine theory can be seen as a context—a relational whole co-emergent between himself or herself and the phenomena of interest. Models co-emerge in this interrelated system of action, reaction, and counter-reaction in a cybernetic causal process. As such, theories can be seen as wholes themselves lent to analysis using the ideas of a wholes approach. This means that the process of science itself is part and parcel of the phenomena of interest.

In light of this it is possible to think about models the same way a wholes approach suggests thinking about anything else. The principles of context, multiverse, and emotion are as useful to the analysis of science as any other phenomena. This makes it possible to shift the question of legitimacy of science to context specificity. Here the question becomes "Does the data fit the theory?" as an emergent property of context, rather than the conventional focus on whether or not the context reflects the universe.

The process of decoding is one of fitting models and data, relative to a scientific context. The wholes approach I present here suggests two main ideas about what the dimensions of fit are and how attention to these dimensions can potentially improve fit—meaning and emotion.

Meaning. The issue of meaning in the science of human groups involves approximating context-specific meaning sets. The question is, "What does something mean to them, the targeted research subjects, in context?" The analytic imperative from a wholes approach is thorny because the subjects themselves may not know what things mean to them in that the whole cannot be found in a part. Because of this the model–data fit, rather than the data from subjects, must become the reference point for judging the salience of a scientific endeavor.

Here all the dimensions of data I outlined above become critical. Without data that captures relational units, sequence, time, and range of behavior, it may not be analytically possible to find the context-specific emergent wholes because they do not exist in the data set.

Decoding to context-specific meaning involves reading data, as related to my criteria for reduction, into a model. Where there is fit, there is the possibility for a general construct. Where there is not fit, it is necessary to revise the model or the data, and likely both, in a feedback process.

In my work on mental illness in intimate relations, this meant beginning with a model of family process (Reiss, 1981). I set about reducing a range of behavior from videotaped interaction samples into data such that the model could be evaluated relative to its fit with the phenomena. However, problems with this reduction process in terms of finding lack of fit prompted me to initially revise Reiss's model and finally replace it with a new model of better fit (Hanson, 1991a). In this process both data and model were refined.

In an organizational context one could think about understanding a targeted problem with productivity, for instance, by trying to unearth what it means to participants. Suppose you researched this in a college in order to understand why the average rates of publication among faculty were dropping. You might discover that the majority of professors are close to retirement and predominantly male. In the junior ranks women predominate. On collecting data from department meetings and focus groups with junior faculty, you discover that there is a strong antipublication rule in the informal interaction practices. While junior women are told formally they should publish, they are burdened with administration and expected to be present in their offices, which detracts from time spent on research. When they do publish, it is not recognized or valued in terms of their job performance. Or if they are strong in publication, senior administrators criticize their teaching. Many junior women faculty leave for other jobs. When new professors are hired or chosen for advanced positions within the college, search committees tend to favor people with less publication over those with more publication. By observing these processes you could detect the unwritten rule against productivity in the face of stated goals of productivity.

Why does no one use this new multimillion dollar community center that was supposed to draw the community together? Decoding data to contextual meaning sets here would involve looking past surface protestations of support to what the center represents to the people who might use it. Here it would be useful to examine critically whose opinions were solicited in terms of selecting a site and format. If it was middle-aged males, while young mothers with breastfeeding babies predominate in the potential market, setting up all activities for 3-hour periods with no facilities for children would mean women would not define it as a place for them. To get at ideas for changes to the center, it might be worthwhile to go out into the surrounding community and observe, even film, the kinds of people and activities that are going on, then adapt the center to this. If you saw dozens of mothers with young children who were bored and fussy, you might set up a situation where mothers could come with children to play or learn in time frames that fit with school and shift work schedules.

In each instance the message is to decode to meaning, not just in the sense of language, but in terms of context-based patterns of understanding which, though not formalized or even conscious, govern behavior. As such these patterns become the target of analysis particularly where intervention is a goal. If an analyst does not understand what governs behavior, he or she cannot hope to change such patterns.

Emotion. In terms of emotion, decoding means being flexible, particularly as regards finding patterns in arrays of shapes and directions that are not found in linear sequences. The suprarational and equi- or multifinal nature of emotion means that its manifestations, detected in data, will show up in nonlinear patterns and in flexible time frames. It is therefore necessary to be sensitive to more fluid representations of phenomena, hand drawings of curves and bounces, rather than computer-simulated regression lines. It is also necessary to reset our analytic mind-set to each case in a data set in order to capture variations in terms of how quickly and with how many actions patterns of emotion manifest.

In my work on mental illness, this meant doing drawings of emotional patterns that reflected what I saw indicated in levels of arousal, either to happiness or anger, in varying time frames. I unearthed the definitional deficit and definitional equality pattern as it played out in families, by being attentive to the ways in which similar patterns of lingering pain or fluid calm showed up in different time frames or different ranges. Figure 5 below shows several variations in terms of how a particular case might show the same pattern, but would have been missed had I assumed a universal time frame or range for arousal.

In an institution one could begin watching a targeted behavior—violent outbursts in nursing homes, for example. Suppose you ultimately discovered a pattern whereby levels of outbursts were linked to residents' recent contact with family members. However, on the way to discerning this pattern you would have to take long time frames into account and compare across cases. In this instance variations in traditional gatherings owing to different religious or cultural backgrounds would cause variations in the pattern such that a seasonal interpretation might be falsely ascribed when violence most often occurred in early fall and early winter. If you did not account for differences between Jewish and Christian traditional gatherings, you could miss the patterns of intense interaction with family members stimulating emotional reactions. Seeing these relations on a more amplified basis, the highest levels all year, could then prompt looking at average levels and seeing if they were related on a case level basis to less intense and more evenly distributed events like birthdays.

The same principle in terms of detecting emotional reactivity relative to varying time frames could be used to guide policies, for instance, on vacation times. This could have been at the heart of instituting "reading weeks" in the early winter of college sessions in response to higher rates of suicide, illness, and

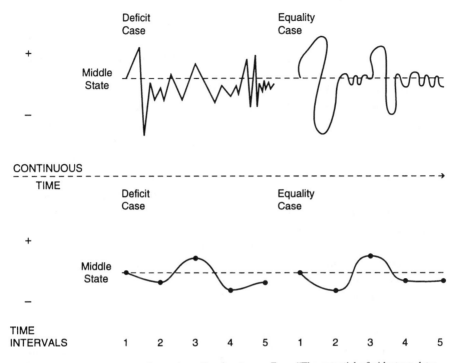

Figure 5 Representing two observed emotional patterns. From "The potential of videotape data: Emotional correlates of senile dementia in families as a case in point," by B. G. Hanson, 1994, *Quality and Quantity*, *28*, p. 226. Copyright 1994 Kluwer Academic Publishers. Reprinted with permission.

depression. By looking through flexible time frames and ranges of emotional arousal as related to specific illness or violent events, the co-emergent effects of intense intimate contact with externally imposed deadlines emerge. A theory that models these elements as exacerbating potentially pathological emotional patterns could then be developed.

The key directive of emotion in decoding is that methods and analysis must be as flexible as the modeled nature of the characteristic of emotion. If it is theorized as nonlinear and equi- or multifinal, we must see in modes both of time and range that allow us to capture it. If the time is too short or the range too small, or the time and range are universalized in a manner that masks individual variation, then emotional patterns will remain outside the viewing lens of analysis.

General Constructs

Perhaps the most radical and controversial implication of my wholes approach is theorizing a basis for legitimacy of scientific advance that is removed from universalism. The construct of multiverse, or realities, which underpins my version of a general systems theory approach, via the assumption of human subjectivity makes it possible to propose particularism, rather than universalism as the reference point for analysis.

By accepting a notion of multiverse, the reference point becomes nonsummative wholes, or contexts. The definition of interrelated parts is as applicable to the phenomena scientist system as to parts in the phenomena being studied. The criteria for success or closure are therefore legitimately defined in terms of a context, be it scientist phenomena or two or more parts in the phenomena.

The issue becomes fit, or validity. Generalization as a criteria is rendered moot by the notion of multiverse. There is nothing to generalize to, beyond the defined context. What is more relevant is clarity relative to the emergent model, such that it can be communicated.

In this sense, analysis is guided toward general constructs that show conceptual consistency within themselves and as they are translated into, and guided by, data. The goal is transportation of such theoretically consistent general constructs to analysis of other contexts. The question is thus shifted from "Is it true?" to "Does it help?" or "Is it useful?"

The criteria for power, relevance, or importance of conclusions of research, are thus legitimately shifted to their contexts of use. A parallogical conception of meaning relative to judgments of sanity allows looking into the particular nature of human contexts that may lead to definition of someone as sick, as separate from posited external diseases or conditions. By the same argument, it is possible to look at judgments of research salience relative to their contexts, as separate from posited external universal laws. Clarity and consistency of constructs, relative to context, becomes the criteria by which science is judged.

CONCLUSION

What is the relevance of wholes thinking in the 1990s? I sense that general systems theory is a mode of thinking with which the world is beginning to catch up. It has been around at least as far back as Aristotle, but has not been fully utilized. Levels of education and public awareness about local and global problems—social, health, and environmental—have never been greater. Current thinking about globalism cries out for a way of seeing the world that does not require first reducing it to mechanical parts. This is as true for you and the people you love as for businesses and organizations and for global social policy. We are beginning to learn that you cannot separate the destruction of the rainforests in South America from the production of Cadillacs in the U.S., from pervasive racism and sexism, or from escalating food bank use. It is time to use theory that takes this irreducible connectedness as its defining principle, or raison d'être.

The whole is greater than the sum of its parts. These wholes, or contexts, become the focus of attention. Because phenomena are connected as emergent wholes, it is important to see that changing one part of a system changes all its parts. Dividing the world into individual parts will miss emergent wholes, making it better to see relationships between parts as the unit of interest.

Within interconnected systems of relationships, causality becomes an issue of what makes things happen or brings things about. Because wholes, which are not seen in individual parts, emerge in systems, they have the ability to regulate or steer themselves. Study of this process of steering is know as cybernetics. Since everything is connected to everything, both action and inaction have equal causal status. It is difficult to assign cause to any single part or action or inaction because they happen in concert, they co-emerge. Blame of one part, action, or inaction is therefore meaningless.

Change becomes a question of what changes and what stays the same. Feedback, the ability of a system to reintroduce input as output or act back upon itself, can lead to change (positive feedback) or no change (negative feedback). Systems, therefore, exhibit emergent properties that are not reducible either to the parts of the system or the nature of the stimuli acting on it. Thus, you can get the same result from any number of different stimuli (equifinality) or an array of different results from the same stimuli (multifinality).

Taking the nonprescriptive language of a wholes approach into the study of human groups involves thinking about what characteristics may be unique or particularly relevant to human, as opposed to mechanical, physical, or biological, systems. Context refers to the emergent whole of any system of two or more parts. Content captures what might be contained in a human context. This involves sensitivity to the human capability to act in concert to develop meanings that are relative to their context of origin, like the Canadian "washroom," the American "restroom," and the British "loo." Because meaning is relative to human joint productions, logic is parallel or parallogical, in the sense that it differs according to what is appropriate in context. This leads to the idea that since human beings act based not on things but rather on the context-specific meanings things have for them, singular reality is less relevant that multiple realities.

Communicating in systems involves an exchange of information. Information can be either about the superficial bits of formal data conveyed in language, reports, or messages, or it can be about the relationship conveyed in nonverbal language, commands. Because everything is related to everything, you cannot not communicate; both silence and talk give information. When there are contradictions between report and command, what is said and what is meant, people are driven crazy by the irresolvability of their situation—a double bind where they can do no right.

Emotion is a higher order, overarching characteristic of human groups that can be seen as a characteristic of relationships rather than individuals. In this sense, it overrides or goes beyond rationality or cognition. Taking a wholes approach into the concrete example of families allows us to see an emotional pattern whereby one family member comes to be considered crazy because they are not involved in the process of defining what is real. This observation at the level of intimacy leads to the idea that social illness categories based on age, sex, and race reflect ageism, sexism, and racism, rather than differences in symptoms.

Moving ahead with a wholes approach means using its language to begin thinking expansively about current concerns: getting a two-year-old child interested in reading, selling more cars, or dealing effectively with AIDS. Concretely this means using a view of science as theory refinement that allows a greater range of theories to be explored. It also encourages analysts to be self-reflexive and consider what aspects of the way they see the world may reflect in certain types of conclusions. Systems alternatives to traditional modes of scientific exploration are found in seeing multiverse rather than universe, emotion as overriding rationality, and subjectivity in equal importance to objectivity. This suggests new ways of conducting scientific study with new tools—an expanded view of data as the relationship between the world and the views of a scientist, decoding information relative to its context, and searching for general constructs in context rather than generalizable findings.

A wholes approach as a way of seeing, rather than a prescriptive theory, promises to change analysis radically because it changes not only what we see but also how we see. New topics and fresh angles on old topics that have never been considered relevant begin to come into focus. Linear thinking leads science on the same linear path. Cybernetic thinking expands the process into a multidimensional task. It is somewhat like moving from still photographs or films to virtual reality simulators that not only move in three dimensions but also give the actor a sense of his or her own efficacy, the ability to change and direct. The scientist as actor seeing from a wholes approach can reflect upon his or her actions and the biases that shape those actions.

Annotated References

Adams, D. (1979/1992). *A hitch hiker's guide to the galaxy: A trilogy in four parts.* London: Heinemann.

American Cancer Society. (1967). *New directions in cancer research.* New York: American Cancer Society.

Ashley, D., & Orenstein, D. M. (1990). *Sociological theory: Classical statements.* Toronto: Allyn and Bacon.

Bateson, G., Jackson, D. D., Haley, J., & Weakland, J. (1956/1976). Towards a theory of schizophrenia. *Behavioral Science, 1,* 251–264.

> A pivotal piece in the development of systems theory in family. Points out the possibility for modes of communication such as what is said and the messages about the verbal communication. This leads into the discussion of double bind, an inescapable situation in which the verbal and messages in other communication (voice tone, sequence, body language, and so on) are not necessarily compatible. It is proposed that these double bind situations are what lead to schizophrenia.

Bertalanffy, L. von. (1968). *General systems theory.* New York: George Braziller, Inc.

> THE book. A major piece in the history of General Systems Theory. Spells out in detail various aspects of systems thinking.

Bertalanffy, L. von. (1975). *Perspectives on general systems theory.* New York: George Braziller.

Blakeley, P. R., & Vernon, M. C. (1963). *The story of Prince Edward Island.* Toronto: J. M. Dent & Sons.

Blumer, H. (1969). *Symbolic interactionism: Perspective and method.* Englewood Cliffs, NJ: Prentice-Hall, Inc.

> A major work on symbolic interactionism. Blumer is credited with originating the term.

Buckley, W. (1967). *Sociology and modern systems theory.* Englewood Cliffs, NJ: Prentice-Hall, Inc.

> The major explication of systems theory as phrased from the viewpoint of the assumptions of sociology. Points out the similarities and differences between modern systems theory and Parsons' model.

Carroll, L. (1865/1981). *Alice's adventures in wonderland and through the looking glass.* Toronto: Bantam Books.

Entries of special interest are accompanied by a brief description.

Checkland, P. B. (1983). Science and the systems movement. In Open Systems Group (Ed.), *Systems behavior* (pp. 26–43). New York: Harper & Row Publishers.

Draws the line from Aristotle to system theory through the link of non-summativity.

Clancy, T. (1986). *Red storm rising*. New York: Putnam.

Cowley, G. (1993, December 6). Family matters: The hunt for a breast cancer gene. *Newsweek,* 46–52.

Darling, C., & Thomson-Delaney, J. (1992). Bluebirds, blowflies, and parasitic wasps. *Rotunda: The Magazine of the Royal Ontario Museum, 25,* (1), 37–40.

De Beauvoir, S. (1949/1989). *The second sex*. New York: Vintage Books.

Emerson, J. (1970). Behavior in private places: Sustaining definitions of reality. In H. P. Dreitzel (Ed.), *Recent Sociology Number 2*. New York: Collier Macmillan.

Faludi, S. (1991). *Backlash*. New York: Crown Publishers, Inc.

Fischer, R. (1985). Deconstructing reality. *Diogenes, 129,* 47–62.

Argues that it is the interactive process between the physical and interpretative that "creates information" (p. 50).

"Fisherman hits jackpot, nets $500,000 bluefin tuna." (1994, September 23). *Toronto Star*, p. A5.

Glasersfeld, E. von. (1984). An introduction to radical constructivism. In P. Watzlawick (Ed.), *The invented reality* (pp. 17–40). New York: W. W. Norton and Company.

Discussion of the nature of constructivism and its social historical context.

Goffman, E. (1961). *Asylums*. New York: Doubleday & Company.

Pioneering piece on the life of mental patients. From a symbolic interactionist perspective, he comes up with a series of ideas that capture the process of becoming a patient and adjusting to life in a mental hospital.

Hanson, B. G. (1985). Negotiation of self and setting to advantage: An interactionist consideration of nursing home data. *Sociology of Health and Illness, 7* (1), 21–35.

Hanson, B. G. (1989a). Definitional deficit: A model of senile dementia in context. *Family Process, 28* (3), 281–289.

Hanson, B. G. (1989b). Parallogic: As mind meets context. *Diogenes, 147,* 77–91.

Hanson, B. G. (1991a). Beyond information processing in families: Modeling and measuring affect as a property of intimate context. *International Journal of Sociology of the Family, 21* (1), 97–109.

Hanson, B. G. (1991b). Conceptualizing contextual emotion: The grounds for "suprarationality." *Diogenes, 156,* 33–46.

Hanson, B. G. (1991c). Parts, players, and "patienting." The social construction of senile dementia. *Family Systems Medicine, 9* (3), 267–274.

Hanson, B. G. (1992). Putting families in family research: Nonsummativity, affect and unit in methodology. *International Journal of Sociology of the Family, 22* (2), 11–29.

Hanson, B. G. (1994a). *The intimate politics of sense*. Manuscript submitted for publication.

Hanson, B. G. (1994b). *Linear causality: The squeaky wheel in the micro–macro debate*. Manuscript submitted for publication.

Hanson, B. G. (1994c). *Out of Control Groups* (under review). New Brunswick, NJ: Rutgers University Press.

Hanson, B. G. (1994d). *Round pegs through square wholes: Constructivist implications for mental illness intervention*. Manuscript submitted for publication.

Hanson, B. G. (1994e). Using videotape to find the emotional correlates of senile dementia in families. *Quality and Quantity, 28,* 219–232.

Hanson, B. G. (in press-a). Human rulers: The constructivist question in reliability based on inter-rater agreement. *Methodology and Science.*

Hanson, B. G. (in press-b). Two minds, two hearts: Questioning inter-rater agreement using emotional data with senile dementia. *Journal of Aging Studies.*

Hardin, G. (1968). The cybernetics of competition: A biologists' view of society. In Walter Buckley (Ed.), *Modern systems research for the behavioral scientist* (pp. 449–459). Chicago: Aldine Publishing Company.

> Interesting discussion of the nature and utility of a systems concept. Excellent example (p.55) of how an abundant supply of "old maids" is the backbone of English society in that they keep cats and this interrelates to horse breeding. Cats eat rats, rats eat bee nests, bees fertilize clover, clover is needed for horses.

Hoffman, F. (1915). *The mortality from cancer throughout the world.* Newark, NJ: The Prudential Press.

Keeney, B. P. (1983). *Aesthetics of Change.* New York: The Guilford Press.

> Discussion of the dynamics of observation and how the observer is part of the subject. An interesting cite of an experiment where Pavlov's experiment was repeated without the bell clapper and the dogs' behavior was unaltered, leading to the conclusion that the bell was a cue for Pavlov, not the dogs.

Kirkland, G., & Lawrence, G. (1986). *Dancing on my grave.* New York: Doubleday & Company Inc.

Kuhn, T. (1970). *The structure of scientific revolutions.* Chicago: University of Chicago Press.

Laing, R. D., & Esterson, A. (1964). *Sanity, madness and the family.* Markham, Ontario: Penguin Books Canada, Ltd.

> Revolutionary treatment of the context of schizophrenia. Detailed case presentations draw the reader into the world of the patient and how "madness" is constructed and maintained in the context of intimate relations.

Lampton, C. (1992). *Science of chaos.* Toronto: Franklin Watts.

> A clearly written and simple discussion of chaos theory, which some think may be the next step in a systems approach by beginning the task of rendering its principles accessible through mathematical computer simulation.

Laurence, M. (1978). *The stone angel.* New York: Bantam Books.

Lewin, K. (1951). *Field theory in social science.* New York: Harper & Brothers.

Lidz, T. (1957). The intrafamilial environment of schizophrenic patients: Marital schism and marital skew. *American Journal of Psychiatry, 114,* 241–248.

> Interesting development of the theory of marital schism (gulf), versus marital skew (distortion to one parent owing to this parent's psychopathology).

Luhmann, N. (1982). *The differentiation of society.* New York: Columbia University Press.

Marshall, J. R., & Neil, J. (1977). The removal of psychosomatic symptom: Effect on the marriage. *Family Process, 16,* 273–280.

> Interesting examination of the nature of marital relationships when the woman undergoes a bowel reduction to reverse extreme obesity. Examines how the relationships are disrupted after the weight loss, calling into question what obesity means in context.

Meakin, J. A. (1979). Hormones as carcinogens in humans. In J. A. Kellen & R. Hilf (Eds.), *Influences of hormones in tumor development.* Boca Raton, FL: CRC Press.

Miller, G. A. (1968). What is information management. In Walter Buckley (Ed.), *Modern systems research for the behavioral scientist* (pp. 123–128). Chicago: Aldine Publishing Company.
Discusses the concept of information in general systems theory terms, including noise.

Montgomery, L.M.(1908/1987). *Anne of Green Gables*(p. 28). Ontario: McGraw-Hill Ryerson, Ltd.

Murphy, J.W. (1988). The relevance of postmodernism for social science. *Diogenes, 143*, 93–110.

Needham, R. (1968). *The garden of Needham.* Toronto: Macmillan Company of Canada.

Niederhe, G., & Fruge, E. D. (1984). Dementia and family dynamics. *Journal of Geriatric Psychiatry, 17*(1).

Ontario Educational Communications. (1985). Toronto: TV Ontario.

Parsons, T. (1979). *The social system.* London: Routledge and Kegan Paul Ltd.
Elaborates a systems model of society using assumptions of evolution, hierarchy, and role. Spells out the concept of "sick role" (p. 436).

Pim, L. R. (1981). *The invisible additives: Environmental contaminants in our food.* Toronto: Doubleday & Company.

Preist, L. (1994, August 9). Fighting the sexy superbugs. *The Toronto Star,* p. A1.

Rapoport, A. (1989). The redemption of science. *Journal of Business Ethics, 8,* 2 & 3, 157–165.
Talks globally about the role of scientists in the development of wars and weaponry. Argues that science will be redeemed by the recognition of the humanness of scientists.

Rapoport, A. (1974). *Conflict in a man-made environment.* Markham, Ontario: Penguin Books.
Spells out theories on peace and conflict. Argues that war be reconceptualized as organized crime.

Reiss, D. (1981). *The family's construction of reality.* Cambridge, MA: Harvard University Press.
Groundbreaking piece that proposes that families have a shared paradigm that is at the base of their modes of decision making and information sharing. A detailed description of the empirical process that went into formulating this construct is included. Develops the dimensions of coordination, configuration, and closure to differentiate types of paradigms. The model is based primarily on the cognitive level focusing on information processing.

Rose, F. (1989). *West of Eden: The end of innocence at Apple.* Markham, Ontario: Penguin Books Ltd.

Rosenhan, D. L. (1976). On being sane in insane places. In D. Krebs (Ed.), *Readings in social psychology* (pp. 281–289). New York: Harper & Row Publishers, Inc.
A major contribution to thinking about mental illness. Chronicles the process whereby people posing as schizophrenia patients enter mental hospitals. Their behavior is interpreted as symptomatic. The only people who detect the "fraud" are other patients. All were discharged with a diagnosis of schizophrenia "in remission."

Shilts, R. (1987). *And the band played on.* New York: St. Martin's Press.

Skinner, B. F. (1948). *Walden two.* New York: Macmillan.

Smith, D. (1987). *The everyday world and problematic.* Toronto: University of Toronto Press.

Sorokin, P. (1957). *Social and cultural dynamics.* Boston: Porter Sargent.

Srole, L., Langner, T. S., Michael, S. T., Kirkpatrick, P., Opler, M. K., & Rennie, T. A. (1978). *Mental health in the metropolis: The midtown manhattan study.* New York: New York University Press.

Study that shows that over half of the people in a random sample of the general population in Manhattan have baseline rates showing significant symptoms of mental illness.

Thomas, W., & Thomas, D. S. (1928). *The child in America.* New York: Alfred A. Knopf.

Tomatis, L. (Ed. in Chief). (1990). *Cancer: Causes, occurrence, and control.* Lyon, France: International Agency for Research on Cancer.

Tomkins, S. (1981). Image, purpose and affect. In F. E. Emery (Ed.), *Systems thinking: 2* (pp. 117–124). Markham, Ontario: Penguin Books Canada, Ltd.

Points out that "[t]he drive system is, however, secondary to the affect system" (p. 122).

Wallace, R. A., & Wolf, A. (1991). *Contemporary sociological theory.* Englewood Cliffs, NJ: Prentice-Hall.

Watzlawick, P., Beavin, J. H., & Jackson, D. D. (1967). *Pragmatics of human communication.* New York: W. W. Norton & Company.

Pivotal piece outlining the basis of an approach to systems with a focus on families and mental illness. Outlines groundbreaking concepts such as report and command and, in so doing, the concept of metacommunication. Develops important axioms of communication and illustration through use of the play "Who's Afraid of Virginia Woolf?"

Wiener, N. (1948). *Cybernetics.* New York: John Wiley & Sons.

THE book on cybernetics that started systems theory in motion. Spells out the basics of the position and its connection to the Greek word "cyber" for steersman. Includes a discussion of the importance of social responsibility for scientific knowledge.

Whyte, W. F. (1943/1981). *Street corner society.* Chicago: University of Chicago Press.

Wynne, L. C., Rycoff, I. M., Day, J., & Hirsch, S. I. (1958). Pseudo-mutuality in the family relations of schizophrenics. *Psychiatry, 21,* 205–220.

Spells out the construct of pseudo-mutuality. "In short, the pseudo-mutual relation involves a characteristic dilemma: Divergence is perceived as leading to disruption of the relation and therefore must be avoided; but if divergence is avoided, growth of the relation is impossible" (p. 207).

Annotated Bibliography

Agnew, N. K., & Brown, J. L. (1986). Bounded rationality: Fallible decisions in unbounded decision space. *Behavioral Science, 31,* 148–161.
 An interesting argument about the inapplicability of rational models of human system behavior to decision making in relevant world issues.
Angyal, A. (1981). A logic of systems. In F. E. Emery (Ed.), *Systems thinking: 1* (pp. 17–29). Markham, Ontario: Penguin Books Canada, Ltd.
 Interesting discussion of the basis of a systems approach.
Asch, S. E. (1981). The individual and the group. In F.E. Emery (Ed.), *Systems thinking: 2* (pp. 138–156). Markham, Ontario: Penguin Books Canada, Ltd.
 Discussion of the mathematical extension of systems thinking, specifically as involves summative math to capture non-summative phenomena.
Ball, R. A. (1978). Sociology and general systems theory. *The American Sociologist, 13,* 65–72.
Bateson, G. (1978).The birth of a matrix or double bind epistemology. In M. M. Berger (Ed.), *Beyond the double bind* (pp. 41–64). New York: Brunner/Mazel Publishers.
Bell, N. W. (1962). Extended family relations of disturbed and well families. *Family Process, 1,* 175–193.
 Uses data to argue the theory that behavior of individuals needs to be seen in relation to families as wholes, including extended family members. Argues that extended relations retain and continue conflicts that existed before marriage.
Bell, N. W. (1986). Metatheories of child abuse. In R. Volpe, M. Breton, & J. Mitton (Eds.), *The maltreatment of the school-aged child* (pp. 171–185). Toronto: D.C. Heath and Company.
 Discusses the historical context of knowledge and how it is socially constructed. Points out the particular dilemmas involved in the human sciences when the observer is part of what is observed.
Berardo, F. M. (1980). Decade preview: Some trends and directions for family research and theory in the 1980s. *Journal of Marriage and the Family, 42,* 723–728.
 A general discussion of the body of theory of family. Specific discussion of the importance of general systems theory and the need to move beyond the descriptive.
Berger, P., & Kellner, H. (1970). Marriage and the construction of reality: An exercise

---

Entries of special interest are accompanied by a brief description.

in the microsociology of knowledge. In M. P. Dreitzel (Ed.), *Recent Sociology, No. 2* (pp. 50–73). New York: Collier Macmillan.

One of the single most important pieces of work on families. This article sets the stage for consideration of a joint relational meaning set developed via marriage.

Blauberg, I. V., Sadovsky, V. N., & Yudin, E. G. (1977). *Systems theory: Philosophical and methodological problems.* Moscow: Progress Publishers.

A sweeping discussion of how systems theory has been applied in various disciplines and in structural functionalism.

Boulding, K. E. (1968). General systems theory—The skeleton of science. In W. Buckley (Ed.), *Modern systems research for the behavioral scientist* (pp. 3–10). Chicago: Aldine Publishing Company.

The basis of a systems approach as focused on levels and hierarchy.

Bowen, M. (1978). *Family therapy in clinical practice.* New York: Jason Aronson Inc.

Broderick, C. (1970). Beyond the five conceptual frameworks: A decade of development in family theory. *National Council on Family Relations, 32,* 3–23.

Overview of the field of theory about families that points out the importance of systems theory and the need for its further development and application.

Brodrick, C., & Smith, J. (1979). The general systems approach to the family. In W. R. Burr, et al. (Eds.), *Contemporary theories about family: General theories/theoretical orientations Volume II* (pp. 112–129). New York: The Free Press.

A description of the basics of systems theory and how it compares with other dominant theories about families.

Bross, A. (1982). *Family therapy: A recursive model of strategic practice.* Toronto: Methuen.

Spells out the basics of systems theory as they relate to the particular therapeutic model of recursive family therapy.

Bross, A., & Benjamin, M. (1982). Family therapy: A recursive model of strategic practice. In A. Bross (Ed.), *Family therapy: A recursive model of strategic practice* (pp. 2–38). Toronto: Methuen.

Detailed discussion of systems theory in a therapeutic setting, relying on notions of hierarchy, goal orientation, and homeostasis.

Buckley, W. (1967). Society as a complex adaptive system. In W. Buckley (Ed.), *Modern systems research for the behavioral scientist* (pp. 490–513). Chicago: Aldine Publishing Company.

Discusses concept of society from a systems view.

Buckley, W. (1968). General introduction. In W. Buckley (Ed.), *Modern systems research for the behavioral scientist* (pp. 490–513). Chicago: Aldine Publishing Company.

Discussion of basics of systems theory as applied to the behavioral sciences.

Cousins, P. C., & Power, T. G. (1986). Quantifying family process: Issues in the analysis of interaction sequences. *Family Process, 25,* (1), 89–105.

A thoughtful and thorough discussion of the issues involved in trying to quantify family interaction processes, notably issues of sequence and varying time frame.

Dell, P. (1986a). In defense of lineal causality. *Family Process, 4,* (25), 513–521.

Interesting discussion of lineal causality. Makes the point that causality is an artifact of the process of description, which inherently involves explanation.

Dell, P. (1986b). Why do we still call them paradoxes? *Family Process, 25,* (2), 223–234.

Presents the paradox in an assumption of objectivity for intervention. Argues that objectivity itself is paradoxical and must be abandoned.

Dreyer, C. A., & Dreyer, A. S. (1973). Family dinner time as a unique behavior habitat. *Family Process, 12,* 291–301.
   Argues for the uniqueness of dinner time for analyzing family behavior in that it is one of the few times all are together. Important for observation of rules and rituals.

Emery, F. E. (1981a). Causal path analysis. In F. E. Emery (Ed.), *Systems thinking: 1* (pp. 293–298). Markham, Ontario: Penguin Books Canada, Ltd.

Emery, F. E. (1981b). The causal structure of organizational environments. In F. E. Emery (Ed.), *Systems thinking: 1* (pp. 245–262). Markham, Ontario: Penguin Books Canada, Ltd.
   Basic systems concepts.

Emery, F. E. (1981c). On hierarchal systems. In F. E. Emery (Ed.), *Systems thinking: 2* (pp. 2–15). Markham, Ontario: Penguin Books Canada, Ltd.
   Argues that hierarchy is not necessary for systems thinking.

Ford, F. R. (1983). Rules: The invisible family. *Family Process, 22,* (2), 135–145.
   Thoughtful discussion of the concept of family rules and their significance.

Frischknecht, F. (1987). Dialogue on information philosophy of behavioral sciences: Positivist bias misses the symbol system point. *Behavioral Science, 32,* 234–237.
   Argues that positivism is no longer tenable for the sciences. Stresses the symbol system point.

Gottman, J. M. (1979). *Marital interaction.* New York: Academic Press.
   Thorough and thoughtful presentation of empirical investigations into family interaction. Detailed discussion of previous work on the subject, what is discovered by the author, and the methodological issues that arose during the investigation.

Grotevant, H., & Carlson, C. I. (1987). Family interaction coding systems: A descriptive review. *Family Process, 26,* (1), 49–74.
   Reviews research in terms of coding systems used relative to theoretical goals. Strategies appear conventional in terms of units.

Haley, J. (1959). The family of the schizophrenic: A model system. *Journal of Nervous and Mental Disease, 129,* 357–374.
   Describes the family situation of schizophrenics in terms of dominant mothers and weak fathers.

Haley, J. (1972). Critical overview of present status of family interaction research. In J. L. Framo (Ed.), *Family interaction* (pp. 13–40). New York: Springer Publishing Company, Inc.
   Reviews recent research and points out the necessity of research that delves into whether or not clinical populations of families differ from normal families.

Hall, A. D., & Fagen, R. E. (1968). Definition of system. In W. Buckley (Ed.), *Modern systems research for the behavioral scientist* (pp. 81–96). Chicago: Aldine Publishing Company.
   Detailed definition of the concept of system.

Hanson, B. G. (1987). *Attempts to model context: Senile dementia in the family as a case demonstration.* Unpublished doctoral dissertation, University of Toronto, Canada.
   Extensive discussion of an empirical experience with families with aged members, some of whom were identified as senile dementia patients. Develops a tentative theory about family types and outlines in detail the methodological issues involved in research using a systems or constructivist approach.

Harris, M. (1981). Mother cow. In F.E. Emery (Ed.), *Systems thinking: 2* (pp. 301–318). Middlesex, England: Penguin Books.
    Examines the role of the sacred cow in Indian society as an example of the inter-relatedness of all elements of a system and the external appearance of illogic.
Hatcher, J. W., Jr. (1987). Arguments for the existence of a general theory of behavior. *Behavioral Science, 32,* 179–189.
    Argues that evolutionary principles of systems can lead to a general theory of behavior.
Holman, T. B., & Burr, W. R. (1980). Beyond the beyond: The growth of family theories in the 1970s. *Journal of Marriage and the Family, 42,* 729–741.
    Discusses the importance of systems theory within the range of theoretical development in theories of families during the 1970s. Points out that systems theory is legitimate in both theory and approach.
Jackson, D. D. (1977). The myth of normality. In P. Watzlawick & J. Weakland (Eds.), *The interactional view* (pp. 157–163). New York: W.W. Norton & Company, Inc.
    Argues that normality is a myth. Challenges clinicians to discard it.
Laszlo, E. (1972). *Introduction to systems philosophy.* New York: Gordon and Breach, Science Publishers.
    Detailed discussion of the basics of systems philosophy and its relevance to the study of human behavior.
Keeney, B. P. (1982). What is an epistemology of family therapy? *Family Process, 21,* 153–168.
    Discussion of the theoretical and philosophical issues involved in describing reality.
Laing, R. D. (1969). *The politics of the family.* London: Tavistock Publications.
Leader, A. (1975). The place of in-laws in marital relationships. *Social Casework, 56,* 486–491.
    Points out that marriage relations are not confined to just the couple; in-laws become part of the pattern as well.
Marx, J. L. (1978). Warm-blooded dinosaurs: Evidence pro and con. *Science, 199* (31), 1424–1426.
    Chronicles the process whereby evidence about the cold- or warm-bloodedness of dinosaurs is argued. Suggests that dinosaurs might have been warm-blooded. It is possible to re-interpret all the available information to reach the opposite of the taken-as-true conventional view of dinosaurs as cold-blooded.
Mendell, D., Cleveland, S. E., & Fisher, S. (1968). A five generation family theme. *Family Process, 7,* 126–132.
    Traces theme patterns through five generations of families who present with problems with a single member.
Miller, J. G. (1965). Living systems: Basic concepts. *Behavioral Science, 10,* 193–237.
    Detailed discussion of some of the basics of general systems theory.
Ntumba, T. (1985). Is there a myth of the myth? *Diogenes, 132,* 116–139.
    Raises the point that the attempt to differentiate myth and truth can itself be seen as a myth in that defining myth presupposes that there is such a thing as truth.
Open Systems Group (Ed.). (1983). *Systems behavior* (3rd ed.). New York: Harper & Row.
    Excellent detailed sourcebook on systems terms and thinking.
Papp, P. (1983). *The process of change.* New York: The Guilford Press.
    Book on therapy with interesting introduction that outlines in fluid prose the basic position of a systems stance.
Pittinger, R. E. (1960). *The first five minutes.* Ithaca: Paul Martineau.
    Discussion of dynamics of method when interviewing.

Pollner, M. & McDonald-Wikler, L. (1985). The social construction of unreality: A case study of a family's attributance of competence in a severely retarded child. *Family Process, 24,* 241–254.
> One of the most significant pieces on context and intimacy to appear in decades. Chronicles the process whereby a family creates and sustains a definition of a severely retarded child as "normal" in the face of massive evidence of pronounced mental illness.

Radley, A. (1988). The social form of feeling. *British Journal of Social Psychology, 27,* 5–18.
> Spells out concept of emotion as resting in the relationship between the individual and society.

Rapoport, A. (1972a). Foreword. In Walter Buckley (Ed.), *Modern systems research for the behavioral scientist* (pp. xxii–xxiii). Chicago: Aldine Publishing Company.
> Globally framed discussion of the nature of systems theory and how it has been used.

Rapoport, A. (1972b). The search for simplicity. In E. Laszlo (Ed.), *The relevance of general systems theory* (pp. 13–30). New York: George Braziller.
> Elegant argument about the search for simplicity concluding with, "Therefore, seek simplicity and distrust it" (p. 30).

Sadovsky, V. N. (1974). Problems of a general systems theory as a metatheory. *Ratio, XVI,* 33–50.
> Discussion of problems and paradoxes in the use of GST as a metatheory. Analysis is underpinned by the notion of hierarchy.

Satir, V. (1967). A family of angels: An interview with Virginia Satir. In J. Hayley & L. Hoffman (Eds.), *Techniques of family therapy* (pp. 97–173). New York: Basic Books Inc.
> Points out how behavior is logical to each family system.

Sutherland, J. W. (1973). *A general systems philosophy for the social and behavioral sciences.* New York: George Braziller.
> Extensive presentation of the basics of systems philosophy.

Thompson, L. & Walker, A. J. (1982). The dyad as the unit of analysis: Conceptual and methodological issues. *Journal of Marriage and the Family, 44* (4), 889–900.
> Discusses the necessity of dyadic units in family analysis.

Tomkins, S. (1965). The biopsychosociality of the family. In A. J. Coale (Ed.), *Aspects of the analysis of family structure* (pp. 102–248). Princeton: Princeton University Press.

Watzlawick, P. (1984a). Effect or cause? In P. Watzlawick (Ed.), *The invented reality* (pp. 63–68). New York: W. W. Norton.
> Discussion of the issues in a construct of linear causality.

Watzlawick, P. (1984b). *The invented reality.* New York: W. W. Norton.
> Edited book of papers on the philosophy of constructivism.

Wiener, N. (1950). *On the human use of human beings.* Boston: Houghton Mifflin Company.
> Discusses issues of human nature in the range of species and modeling. Highlights language as a key differentiator.

White, M. (1983). Anorexia nervosa: A transgenerational system perspective. *Family Process, 22* (3), 255–273.
> Spells out the concept that belief patterns in families translate into anorexia events in one member for generations.

Index

Diabetes

Editor

PAUL J. KIM

CLINICS IN PODIATRIC MEDICINE AND SURGERY

www.podiatric.theclinics.com

Consulting Editor
THOMAS J. CHANG

July 2019 • Volume 36 • Number 3

ELSEVIER

1600 John F. Kennedy Boulevard • Suite 1800 • Philadelphia, Pennsylvania, 19103-2899

http://www.theclinics.com

CLINICS IN PODIATRIC MEDICINE AND SURGERY Volume 36, Number 3
July 2019 ISSN 0891-8422, ISBN-13: 978-0-323-68206-0

Editor: Lauren Boyle
Developmental Editor: Laura Kavanaugh

Clinics in Podiatric Medicine and Surgery (ISSN 0891-8422) is published quarterly by Elsevier Inc., 360 Park Avenue South, New York, NY 10010-1710. Months of issue are January, April, July, and October. Business and Editorial Offices: 1600 John F. Kennedy Blvd., Ste. 1800, Philadelphia, PA 19103-2899. Customer Service Office: 3251 Riverport Lane, Maryland Heights, MO 63043. Periodicals postage paid at New York, NY and additional mailing offices. Subscription prices are $304.00 per year for US individuals, $574.00 per year for US institutions, $100.00 per year for US students and residents, $382.00 per year for Canadian individuals, $693.00 for Canadian institutions, $439.00 for international individuals, $693.00 per year for international institutions and $220.00 per year for Canadian and foreign students/residents. To receive student/resident rate, orders must be accompanied by name of affiliated institution, date of term, and the *signature* of program/residency coordinator on institution letterhead. Orders will be billed at individual rate until proof of status is received. Foreign air speed delivery is included in all *Clinics* subscription prices. All prices are subject to change without notice. POSTMASTER: Send address changes to *Clinics in Podiatric Medicine and Surgery*, Elsevier Health Sciences Division, Subscription Customer Service, 3251 Riverport Lane, Maryland Heights, MO 63043. **Customer Service: 1-800-654-2452 (US). From outside of the US, call 314-447-8871. Fax: 314-447-8029. E-mail: JournalsCustomerService-usa@elsevier.com (for print support); JournalsOnlineSupport-usa@elsevier.com (for online support).**

Reprints. For copies of 100 or more of articles in this publication, please contact the Commercial Reprints Department, Elsevier Inc., 360 Park Avenue South, New York, NY 10010-1710. Tel.: 212-633-3874; Fax: 212-633-3820; E-mail: reprints@elsevier.com.

Clinics in Podiatric Medicine and Surgery is covered in *MEDLINE/PubMed (Index Medicus) and EMBASE/Excerpta Medica.*

Printed in the United States of America.

Contributors

CONSULTING EDITOR

THOMAS J. CHANG, DPM
Clinical Professor and Past Chairman, Department of Podiatric Surgery, California College of Podiatric Medicine, Faculty, The Podiatry Institute, Redwood Orthopedic Surgery Associates, Santa Rosa, California

EDITOR

PAUL J. KIM, DPM, MS
Vice Chair of Research, Plastic and Reconstructive Surgery, MedStar Health Inc, Professor, Department of Plastic Surgery, Georgetown University School of Medicine, Washington, DC

AUTHORS

STEVEN ABRAMOWITZ, MD
Assistant Professor of Surgery, Georgetown University, Department of Vascular Surgery, MedStar Washington Hospital Center, Washington, DC

DAVID M. ARONOFF, MD, FIDSA, FAAM
Professor, Division of Infectious Diseases, Departments of Medicine, and Pathology, Microbiology and Immunology, Vanderbilt University Medical Center, Nashville, Tennessee

CHRISTOPHER E. ATTINGER, MD, FACS
Professor, Department of Plastic and Reconstructive Surgery, Director, Center for Wound Healing, MedStar Georgetown University Hospital, Washington, DC

CAROL DEANE BENEDICT MITNICK, MD
Assistant Professor of Medicine, Division of Rheumatology, Immunology and Allergy, Center for Wound Healing, MedStar Georgetown University Hospital, Washington, DC

KAVITHA BHAVAN, MD
Department of Orthopaedic Surgery, The University of Texas Southwestern Medical Center, Dallas, Texas

CARA K. BLACK, BA
Department of Plastic and Reconstructive Surgery, MedStar Georgetown University Hospital, Washington, DC

CODY A. CHASTAIN, MD
Assistant Professor, Division of Infectious Diseases, Department of Medicine, Vanderbilt University Medical Center, Nashville, Tennessee

BRETT C. CHATMAN, DPM, AACFAS
Department of Surgery, Division of Plastic and Reconstructive Surgery, Hospital of the
University of Pennsylvania, Philadelphia, Pennsylvania

STEPHEN CLEMENT, MD
Medical Director, Endocrinology, Department of Medicine, Inova Fairfax Hospital,
Falls Church, Virginia

PETER A. CRISOLOGO, DPM
Assistant Instructor, Department of Plastic Surgery, The University of Texas Southwestern
Medical Center, Dallas, Texas

KAREN KIM EVANS, MD, FACS
Department of Plastic and Reconstructive Surgery, MedStar Georgetown University
Hospital, Washington, DC

KENNETH L. FAN, MD
Department of Plastic and Reconstructive Surgery, MedStar Georgetown University
Hospital, Washington, DC

JAVIER LA FONTAINE, DPM, MS
Professor, Department of Plastic Surgery and Orthopaedic Surgery, The University of
Texas Southwestern Medical Center, Dallas, Texas

TIMOTHY GREENE, DPM
Resident, Temple University Hospital Podiatric Surgical Residency Program, Philadelphia,
Pennsylvania

TODD A. HASENSTEIN, DPM
Resident, Temple University Hospital Podiatric Surgical Residency Program, Philadelphia,
Pennsylvania

LELAND JAFFE, DPM, FACFAS, CWSP
Assistant Professor, Department of Medicine and Radiology, Dr. William M. Scholl
College of Podiatric Medicine at Rosalind Franklin University, North Chicago, Illinois

KELLY JOHNSON-ARBOR, MD, FACEP, FUHM, FACMT
Assistant Professor of Plastic Surgery and Emergency Medicine, MedStar Georgetown
University Hospital, Washington, DC

NATHAN KLOPFENSTEIN, BSc
Division of Infectious Diseases, Departments of Medicine, and Pathology, Microbiology
and Immunology, Vanderbilt University Medical Center, Nashville, Tennessee

VIKAS S. KOTHA, BS
Department of Plastic and Reconstructive Surgery, Research Scholar, Center for Wound
Healing, MedStar Georgetown University Hospital, Washington, DC

TRAPPER LALLI, MD
Assistant Professor, Department of Orthopaedic Surgery, The University of Texas
Southwestern Medical Center, Dallas, Texas

LAWRENCE A. LAVERY, DPM, MPH
Professor, Departments of Plastic Surgery and Orthopaedic Surgery, The University of
Texas Southwestern Medical Center, Dallas, Texas